F·E·E·D
THE
BIRDS

F·E·E·D

THE

BIRDS

By
Helen Witty & Dick Witty

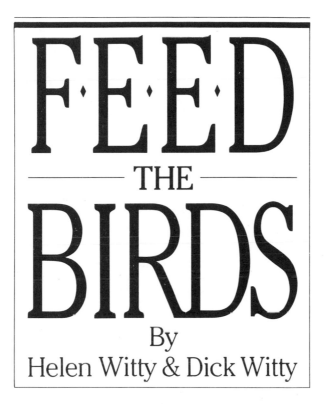

Linocut illustrations by
Stephen Alcorn

WORKMAN PUBLISHING, NEW YORK

✦

Library of Congress Cataloging-in-Publication Data

Witty, Helen.
Feed the birds / Helen Witty & Dick Witty.
p.   cm.
Includes index.
ISBN 1-56305-085-4 (pbk.)
1. Birds—Feeding and feeds. 2. Birds—Food. 3. Bird Feeders.
4. Birds—North America—Feeding and feeds. 5. Birds—North
America—Food.   I. Witty, Dick.   II. Title.
QL676.5.W5   1991
598′.07234—dc20   91-50388
CIP

Cover illustration: Seymour Chwast
Renderings by Jo Tomallo

✦

Workman books are available at special discounts when
purchased in bulk for premiums and sales promotions
as well as for fund-raising or educational use. Special
editions or book excerpts can also be created to
specification. For details, contact the Special Sales Director
at the address below.

Workman Publishing
708 Broadway
New York, New York 10003

Manufactured in the United States of America
First printing September 1991
10   9   8   7   6   5   4

C·O·N·T·E·N·T·S

The Pleasure of Their Company

◆

Who are we, you may ask, to be encouraging you not only to feed the birds but to do a little casual cookery for them, too? Well, experts we're not, but enthusiasts we certainly are, taking ever increasing pleasure in the wild fliers around us — both in the backyard dining area we maintain for them and in the whole wide neighborhood around.

For this excursion into catering for bird guests, your host is the feeder-engineer and commissary officer of our birds' dining area, and your hostess is the chief cook (and scribe). We've been living full-time in the country for seven or eight years now, after decades of working in Manhattan with only weekends and chunks of summertime for breathing deep among the woods and waters of eastern Long Island. Now we're year-rounders, not just summer people, and we're all for the birds ... birds that become more numerous, both in kinds we can identify and in total numbers, the more we read about (and feed) them.

Our Place

The area of the South Fork of Long Island where we live is about 20 miles from the island's eastern tip, beyond which there's only the ocean until you get to Portugal. We're right on the Atlantic flyway, a main north-south migration route for innumerable species, so in spring and fall the doings of the many all-year birds are eclipsed by great flurries of long-haul transients and arriving or departing nesters — all delighting us and the many devoted "birders" who come out to observe them in the wide range of habitats the area affords. Many of the arriving summer sojourners are, to us, becoming old friends.

Our local habitats include wide ocean beaches backed

with grassy dunes, pebbly bay beaches merging into scrubby sand plains, shellfish-rich shallow bays with tidal flats, and salt marshes where ospreys are nesting again after years of near-wipeout by DDT. There are belts of fertile farmland, oak woodlands on sandy soil, and quite a lot of residential landscape resulting from the building of new houses in a resort area. (On the bright side of "development" in an area such as ours, where native plant species are relatively few, good home plantings introduce additional kinds of trees, shrubs and food plants to the environment, all of which may in the long run be a plus.)

Our modest "life list" of birds that come here lengthens season by season. As of today we've identified almost 80 species, including a young bald eagle. We have a small collection of binoculars and a larger one of field guides and handbooks and we've learned delightful things about "our" birds. We don't pretend to know all there is to know, but we can tell you what works for us.

For several years now we've been supplementing the usual feeder offerings of seed, grain and suet with extra snacks and mixtures of our own making. Easy to concoct and keep on hand, these "recipe" foods add choice that brings more birds to our yard at any given time (including some that wouldn't normally venture) and they also contribute useful nutrients. They're all easy enough for non-Cordon Bleu cooks, take little time to do, and in most cases can be customized to suit the preferences of your bird visitors or to make use of what you have in the cupboard.

Getting to Know Them

To get a handle on which bird is which, the first step is to acquire one of the excellent field guides now available. Our advice is to compare field guides by library borrowing or bookstore browsing before you make a choice, since you may well find one to be more appealing than another.

After you've chosen a field guide, consider a bird handbook and a regional guide (or bird list) with the lowdown on which birds you can expect where you live. Regional guides are invaluable because no field guide covering either the East or the West, much less the entire country, can be comparably specific about birds' ranges. Then there are the bird magazines, several enchanting bird videos, and tapes of bird songs to help tune your ear—all a pleasure to have and learn from.

A birders' shop, if one is within reach, and mail-order dealers are reliable sources for books, feeders, birdhouses and birdbaths, just for openers, plus other items educational and frivolous alike, all dealing with or inspired by the birds.

Catering for All Seasons

If you establish a dining area with one or more feeding places, ideally all of the "big four" (ground, table or window shelf, free-hanging feeders, and feeders fixed on tree trunks or posts), and serve a canny choice of foods, you're sure of bringing "feeder" species close to you for watching. Perhaps there will be only a few birds at first, but the word spreads fast. You can observe from indoors (big windows help), a porch, or a chair on the lawn, and you'll be all the better prepared to make bird-spying expeditions beyond the yard to meet the species that are unlikely to come to you.

Your hospitality will keep some birds coming in every season if you'll take our advice (and that of the experts) and offer a spring and summer menu as well as winter food. The cold season is rightly seen as the time of year when resident birds most often need extra food for bare survival; some, such as chickadees, are in real danger of freezing at night if they can't stoke up by almost constant feeding during the day. But spring can be a very hungry time, too, because natural foods are still scarce then, before seeds develop and insects fly and caterpillars crawl.

Although summer offers more wild food than spring, it's also the time when nesters are hard-pressed to nourish their clamoring young as well as themselves, and your food (including "baby" foods) will vanish even faster than usual. Summer catering has another reward—the delight of watching young birds learn to find their own food where their parents have dined before them.

Backyard Beginnings

Before we succeeded in becoming host and hostess with the mostest to our fly-in friends (well, the mostest on our road, anyway), we found we needed to know something about the diners we might expect and what they might like best to eat.

We learned (and books were helpful) that even the tiniest bird needs a lot of food. Feeding is the birds' principal occupation apart from migrating, nesting and rearing young, all activities that in turn increase the need for food hunting. All birds' energy (hence food) requirements are high, and the metabolic rates of some are amazing. The hummingbirds win the prize, with a basal rate about a hundred times that of an elephant. Hummingbirds need to consume approximately their own body weight in nectar every day, plus insects and spiders and such, which are needed to supply protein.

We also learned that birds are opportunistic diners, switching to a new food source when it becomes available, then switching again, whether next week or next year, when the supply runs out or something better appears. We found out for ourselves that the first feeder put out in a yard may not be discovered for a while, and that this can also be true of a new food in an added feeder. For instance, niger (thistle) seed, fancied greatly by goldfinches and a few others, sat in our new tube feeder for weeks before the house finches caught on, although they were taking sunflower seed from a holder a few feet away. It took even longer for the goldfinches to flash into sight and find the niger seed, but once they found it they were hooked.

Just as they change feeding locations (checking old spots, however, just in case), birds will switch menus with flawless opportunism. In diet, few backyard birds seem to be specialists; most subsist on a mixed fare of seed/grain, insects, caterpillars, fruit, even flowers, rather than any single food. So we see nominal seed-eaters take nips from a suet cake, especially if we've thoughtfully included sunflower seed or peanuts in the fatty matrix. In nesting season, even "vegetarian" birds take animal food for the fat and protein; and switch-feeding, of one kind or another, is common all year.

When birds do begin to come to a feeder, don't expect them to feed for a bit, then hang around until they're ready for the next course. Having stayed a rather short time, singly or in a bustling flock and with a sharp eye out for predators, they'll be off to the next stop on a round that includes sources of wild foods as well as other feeders. The busiest periods, usually several a day, become predictable; clearly, birds dine out on a schedule.

A Little of Everything, Please . . .

The nutritional needs of winged creatures are suprisingly like those of humans: fat and carbohydrates for energy, proteins for building and maintaining their bodies and reproducing successfully, and minerals and vitamins for all the same reasons they're needed by people. In addition, birds require a lot of calcium to ensure adequate shells for their eggs. (You'll notice we discuss crushed eggshells as both a desirable side dish and a recipe ingredient.) In nesting season, a generous nearby food supply helps birds rear their broods with less travel and a better chance of success than they'd experience in a less hospitable spot.

Most birds are mainly omnivorous, feeding on animal life of one kind or another as well as seeds, grain, flowers, fruit, and even green stuff; the balance of elements changes from species to species and from season to season in the birds' year. Omnivorous birds increase their intake of protein (from insects, spiders, snails and whatever) in breeding season.

Even the few species that are mainly herbivorous will up their consumption of bugs at nesting time because of their need for protein; birds that are mainly carnivores become entirely so at that season. The nectar-sippers (hummingbirds, orioles, some warblers), too, routinely eat insects and other tiny meaty things to balance their diet of energy-rich but zero-protein flower nectar.

No hard-and-fast list of "right" dining-area foods can be compiled for any bird species, which is why so many food likings are listed for each of the bird groups in "Look

Who's Coming to Dinner." Among those preferences, some may be "right" in one locality or season but not in another; and, too, more food possibilities exist than we could ever list. It's no cause for surprise if a bird raids food intended for an entirely different species or if a "favorite" food is ignored. (Observers' reports astonish and amuse with their notes of the odd eats some birds have been seen to take.)

So it's a sound notion to experiment with various seed and grain mixtures, with "recipe" foods to supply additional nutrients, and with impromptu items including leftovers. You don't have to settle for bags of premixed bird food, unless you prefer.

Building a Guest List

When your first feeder begins to work its wiles, you'll soon find yourself welcoming more than one species. Shortly after our beginnings many winters ago with a rustic wooden hanging feeder (ultimately converted into matchsticks by the squirrels), we noticed that seed spilled by the purple finches, our first visitors, was not going to waste. Mourning doves, blackbirds and cardinals gravitated to the spot to feast, prompting us to strew corn and seed on the ground just for them. In turn, ring-necked pheasants and quail came, too, and meanwhile we'd added one more feeder, then another . . . hanging, standing, tacked to trees, or fastened to windows.

In general it's the larger birds — pheasants, doves, quail, crows, blackbirds, cardinals, robins and towhees, but also some of the sparrows — that prefer to keep their feet on the ground or on a low feeding table. However, some of the "ground" birds can be surprisingly agile, and quite comical, when trying to steal a mouthful from a hanging seed or suet feeder not meant for them.

The tree-clingers, except for the occasional flicker or red-bellied woodpecker that likes to roam at ground level, will seldom dine anywhere but at the trunk of a tree (wild food) or a feeder attached to it (your food). Many tree-clingers, especially downy and hairy woodpeckers, will also visit hanging feeders holding suet or suety mixtures.

Nuthatches, titmice and chickadees, as well as

Carolina wrens, among others, are switch-hitters. They visit seed feeders, suet and suety foods, the morsels on the bird table, and even ground food that looks good to them.

In general, the great middling class of seed-eaters (including such ground birds as cardinals and doves), as well as those birds (such as mockingbirds and catbirds) that like fruit or offbeat snacks, are best accommodated on a feeding table or shelf. Smaller seed-eaters, in their multitudes (many finches, grosbeaks, pine siskins, redpolls, etc.), are pleased with hanging or post-mounted feeders and with offerings on the table or window shelf as well, although they'll picnic on the ground if they must.

"Here we stand like birds in the wilderness, waiting to be fed . . . "

Befriending birds does more than please the bird-friend. Something (more than a *little* something) toward bird survival is being done by those among us who help by supplying, right where we live, the four things that birds must have: food, water, a nesting spot, and shelter from weather and predators. Deprived of habitat by cities, suburbs, one-crop agriculture, deforestation and pollution, bird populations are noticeably dwindling. Many migrant birds make the long flight to old nesting grounds being suburbanized under asphalt, non-nutritious lawns, and shopping malls, only to find less food, less shelter, less of everything they need, which means still fewer birds in our future.

Increasingly, thoughtful people are realizing that the wild resources of Earth are shrinking fast and the bell is tolling more and more frequently for life forms that can never be restored once they're gone. The threat isn't just in the birds' tropical wintering grounds, where environment is being destroyed so fast; it's felt all over the wide areas of North America that are the birds' normal migratory stopovers or destinations. Loss of habitat right in our own backyards may go on almost imperceptibly (to us), but the birds are noticing.

Meanwhile here we are at our place, sharing space with land birds and tree birds, dune birds and bay, perchers and climbers and swimmers, soloists and flockers. Some glean, some drill for food in trees, some catch insects on the wing. The robins hop, heads cocked, watching for signs of the early worm. Some are peaceful souls — we remember especially the purple finches that used to come in quiet flocks, far gentler birds than the pushy, brawling, but endearing house finches who have taken over the territory here and in much of the East. For timid and polite, you can't beat the tufted titmouse, with his big, black, round eye and sporty cap. Phlegmatic? That's the downy woodpecker, a fellow who will sit quietly glued to a suet feeder even when a hawk sails through the area in search of dinner. Cardinals, too, are peaceable souls, quick to yield to bird bullies such as grackles, unlike the unbothered doves that often share the bullies' browsing ground. Droll, henlike scratching among fallen leaves marks the food search of towhees and white-throated sparrows, who make a ruckus out of proportion to their size. Gobblers? Those are the jays, in a dead heat with the blackbird tribe for speed-eating honors.

This is our joy — seeing the birds close up as they come to feed, watching their goings-on, hearing their song. We hope this little book will help you tempt guests to your own backyard so that you, too, can enjoy the pleasure of their company.

Look Who's Coming to Dinner

Somewhere in America, at least one representative of each of the kinds of birds listed here is a feeder visitor — frequent, or fairly frequent, or merely occasional, in large numbers or small. (For our purposes, "feeder" is shorthand for a feeding station, or environment, offering water and nourishment on the ground and/or on feeding tables or shelves and in hanging or fixed feeders of various sorts.) So, regardless of your region, some of these birds we discuss are prospective drinkers of your water and eaters of your seed, suet and other viands.

Some of the birds that follow are seen at feeders relatively rarely and in fortunate yards only (think of orioles, tanagers, most of the warblers), whereas others (finches, jays, doves, blackbirds, various sparrows) may be near-ubiquitous. The list doesn't include birds that guidebooks call "accidentals" and "escapes" — creatures seen outside their usual range because of freak winds or weather, or because they've made a jailbreak from a cage.

Which Birds Where?

The kinds of birds you can expect to come to your feeder will depend on both your general region (North, South, East,

66Take the first step in ornithology . . . and you are ticketed for the whole voyage. . . . Secrets lurk on all sides. There is news in every bush.99
— John Burroughs' America

West) and the local geography and topography. A low desert in the West isn't frequented by the same species as the high Sierras only a few miles away, though both habitats are in the "West"—in fact, in the Far West, a subregion—and are inhabited by "western" birds. Similarly, on the eastern seaboard, a backyard bordering on a saltwater marsh will entertain a different set of birds from those found in the deciduous woodland only a short distance upslope and inland. For instance, we live near the Atlantic beaches and a sheltered bay, but because of our immediate woodsy surroundings we were visited this past winter by more than two dozen species of the birds that like woodlands and semi-open country, including bobwhites, hawks and pheasants. (In summer, there are even more kinds to be seen and, if we're lucky, to be fed.) But only a short walk away the marshes and bay beaches are inhabited, in season, by a different cast of characters—herons, egrets, ospreys, horned larks, swans, plovers, terns, gulls, red-winged blackbirds, ducks, sandpipers and many other water's-edge foragers. Half a mile makes quite a difference.

*'Tis always morning
somewhere, and
above
The awakening
continents, from
shore to shore,
Somewhere the
birds are singing
evermore.*
—*Longfellow, "The Birds of Killingworth," in* Tales of a Wayside Inn

Guidance to Seek

To learn which species you can attract in your locality, consult the notes and range maps in a good field guide or regional guide (page 138). Talk to bird-feeding neighbors and any expert spotters you know. "Bird people" love to share lore; there's no excitement like that felt among birders when a young bald eagle perches in a backyard tree (it happened in our own backyard), or when an unfamiliar species is identified pecking at a feeder. Our first migrating rose-breasted grosbeak kept us beaming for a week.

Backyard Birds & a Few of Their Favorite Foods

In the list that follows, a bird name in capital letters within an entry indicates that the bird has its own separate entry. The foods given for each group are suggestions — good bets but not necessarily preferred by every species in that group. In fact, the food that's most successful in attracting any particular bird can vary from place to place.

BLACKBIRDS. There are six North American species of birds commonly called blackbirds, plus a number of relatives in the same subfamily (the New World blackbirds and orioles), such as GRACKLES and COWBIRDS. The melodious male redwings, with their memorable arrivals in single-sex springtime flocks, are the most striking of the blackbirds, thanks to their epaulets of scarlet and gold. All blackbirds are essentially ground feeders, but individuals will attempt quite comically to land on hanging feeders meant for smaller birds. *Cracked corn, mixed seed, millet; occasionally nutmeats.*

BLUEBIRDS, though infrequent feeder visitors, may turn up occasionally in summer and are worth watching for in the countryside. In the East, look for the eastern bluebird; west of the 100th meridian, you'll find the western and mountain bluebird species. The declining population of these sky-colored beauties is benefiting from the house-building carried out by bluebird lovers in order to combat loss of habitat. *Suet, dried fruit (especially raisins), nutmeats, peanut hearts, baked goods.*

❝*When Nature made the bluebird she wished to propitiate both the sky and the earth, so she gave him the color of the one on his back and the hue of the other on his breast...*❞
—John Burroughs' America

BOBWHITES (NORTHERN BOBWHITES). *See* QUAIL.

BROWN CREEPERS. The bark of living trees, often rich in resident insects and grubs, is the feeding ground of this shy little tree-climbing bird, the only North American member of the creeper group. When a creeper is seen spiraling up the trunk of a tree that has a suet feeder attached, chances are it's searching for fallen crumbs of fat lodged in the bark as well as insects. You can help it feast by smearing chopped or rendered suet right onto the bark of several trees—this worked so well for us that our resident creeper has graduated to visiting the suet holders also.

BUNTINGS. These brilliant tropics-wintering insect-eaters may, in some fortunate regions, patronize a feeder holding small seed such as niger (thistle), canary or millet, or nut or sunflower meats. The five North American bunting species (New World buntings) include the indigo (East), lazuli (West) and painted (South and Southwest). Another group (the New World sparrows) are the Old World buntings, which include the snow bunting, a bird seen in the North in winter flocks that sometimes take seed or grain in places that are open enough to suit their notions.

CARDINALS (NORTHERN CARDINALS), among the most brilliant of red birds, are related to the pyrrhuloxias (cardinal-like desert scrub birds), the dickcissels, and certain grosbeaks and buntings. Divide the United States by a line slanting from the southern tip of California northeast to the Great Lakes and beyond to the Canadian Maritimes and you have, east of the line, the cardinal's range. Within this area,

GONE ROAMING

It's midwinter in snow country and for two days there have been few or no guests at your good-food buffet. Why?

Chances are the birds' absence comes during a mild and sunny spell that encourages them to visit other parts of their normal range to find food (and water, too) that's unobtainable during freeze-ups and when snow is on the ground. They'll be back, and their return may be dramatically sudden when they sense that a storm is on the way. Our birds seem to positively stock up just before bad weather, doing a lot of quarreling as they eat all they can hold.

the cardinal is one of the Big 10 favorite visitors. It takes provender from the ground or feeding tables. *Sunflower seed, safflower seed, cracked corn, millet, shelled or unshelled peanuts, melon and squash seeds, nutmeats, raisins, apples, baked goods; occasionally suet.*

CATBIRDS, more formally gray catbirds, are friendly shrub-haunters that keep an eye on who's putting out the soaked raisins (or other mockingbird-type foods) on the feeding shelf today. These cousins of THRASHERS and MOCKINGBIRDS do indeed "mew" in a catlike fashion. *Dried fruit (especially soaked raisins), sugar water, fresh fruit, suet, nutmeats, cornbread.*

CHICKADEES, known in six North American species, are most familiar in their black-capped, Carolina, mountain and chestnut-backed guises. They're among the most diligent and endearing visitors to hanging feeders (the more tipping and swinging, the better) or feeding tables, often in company with their cousins the TITMICE. *Sunflower seed (especially black-oil sunflower), sunflower meats, shelled peanuts and peanut hearts, niger (thistle), nutmeats, suet, suet or peanut-butter mixtures, baked goods.*

COWBIRDS, members of the tribe of the BLACKBIRDS, are found throughout the contiguous United States. Most common are the brown-headed cowbirds. These small ground feeders are notorious for laying their eggs cuckoo-fashion in the nests of other birds (even those of tiny ones), which then bring up the big, greedy young while the egg-layer and her mate take life easy. *Mixed seed, millet, canary, milo, cracked corn.*

The birds chant melody on every bush;
The green leaves quiver with the cooling wind,
And make a chequer'd shade on the ground.
—*Shakespeare,* Titus Andronicus, *Act II*

CROWS. The four species found in North America belong to a family that includes JAYS, ravens, jackdaws and MAGPIES. They're intelligent and extremely wary birds that keep one eye cocked for any shadow of danger while they're ground-foraging for cracked corn and sunflower seed. As insect-eaters and natural scavengers, they also devour table scraps, especially meat, and suet.

DOVES. This cooing tribe is known in North America in 16 species, one of them given over to the ubiquitous "city" pigeon (rock dove). Others are the mourning, ground, ringed turtle-dove, white-winged and common ground dove, all looking for food mostly at ground level. However, if it's to be found higher up, as on a bird table, doves will find it. *Niger (thistle), millet, sunflower, canary, safflower seeds; cracked corn, milo, nutmeats, peanuts, peanut hearts.*

ENGLISH SPARROWS. *See* SPARROWS.

FINCHES, with about 19 North American species, are most often represented at feeders by house finches (males with orange-red markings) and purple finches (males with raspberry-red markings). Other feeding station species are rosy and Cassin's finches, GOLDFINCHES, pine and evening GROSBEAKS, REDPOLLS, and PINE SISKINS. *Sunflower meats and seed, niger (thistle), suet mixtures, canary, millet, safflower seed, peanut hearts, nutmeats, oranges and other fruit, melon seeds.*

FLICKERS (NORTHERN FLICKERS), belonging to the great grouping of WOODPECKERS, are brilliant in flight because of their underwing color, which varies from race to race although they're a single species.

"In all New England there is no shrewder Yankee than the crow.**"**
—*Bradford Torrey,*
Birds in the Bush

The red-shafted race is found west of the Rockies, the yellow-shafted in the East, and the gilded in the Southwest. They're not routine visitors to feeders, but they sometimes investigate hanging suet feeders or ground stations, and they come for drinks at birdbaths during freeze-ups or drought. *Also: peanut-butter mixtures, nutmeats, grain, various seeds, peanut hearts, fruit.*

GOLDFINCHES. The American and lesser goldfinches are widely distributed FINCHES; another species, Lawrence's, has a limited southwestern and western range. Attracting these charming golden birds is the heart's desire of many, and niger (thistle) seed is often the key. A season or more may pass before goldfinches discover your offering. Best bet in goldfinch country: have your thistle seed and sunflower meats out and on offer well before their springtime arrival. Once they've found the delicacies, they'll be back. *Also: sunflower seed, peanut hearts, millet, suet, suet mixtures.*

GRACKLES. Like them or think them noisy/greedy, these big BLACKBIRDS, with their iridescent heads and shoulders of royal blue, violet, or deep green, are likely to turn up in spring almost anywhere, often in mixed flocks with other blackbirds and the odd STARLING. They scavenge from ground or table, eating almost anything any other bird will touch. Grackle goings-on are entertaining: courtship behavior includes fluffing up to spectacular size; "pecking order" is asserted by bill-tilting — craning the neck to look high into heaven. Grackles also indulge in "anting," one of the strangest of bird displays, involving a wallowing treatment of the feathers with living ants or other odd materials.

PITCHING WOO

And then there's courtship. Besides singing, a lot goes on. Doves will bow to their ladies and coo by the hour; male cardinals, jays, chickadees and titmice feed tidbits to their mates with delicate care; woodpeckers drum an enticing tattoo on a surface chosen for its resonance; the grackle fluffs his feathers until he appears the size of a small turkey, often to be ignored completely by the female of his choice. Other birds, other behaviors, all fascinating to see.

Sunflower seed, cracked corn, canary seed, peanuts, peanut hearts, table scraps.

GROSBEAKS. The six North American species of grosbeaks are not all closely related, but are grouped together because they are all large-billed seed-eaters. The evening, black-headed and rose-breasted grosbeaks will visit feeding stations; rarer feeder visitors are blue and pine grosbeaks. With varying enthusiasm, according to species, grosbeaks feed on *sunflower seed, suet, mixed seed, safflower seed, peanut hearts and meats, millet and other small seeds, nutmeats, cracked corn; occasionally fruit and stolen hummingbird nectar.*

HAWKS. Although hawks don't come to feeders, some may pass over (or through) feeder areas to dine (if they can make a capture) on feeder guests. Hawks are fascinating to observe; they're not a menace that would justify shutting down feeders because small birds know very well how to protect themselves by swift escape or hiding, so only a very occasional capture is made. (Most hawks actually depend on small game such as rodents, frogs and even big insects.)

HORNED LARKS. These are open-country birds, not semi-tame backyard types. Our own local population inhabits a pebbly beach, but they could just as well have chosen nearby fields. In snowy weather these birds sometimes join foraging flocks of other overwintering birds in search of grain and seed in open areas.

HOUSE SPARROWS. *See* SPARROWS.

HUMMINGBIRDS. Of the close to 20 hummingbird species that have been found in North America, nearly all are found in the

THE EYES HAVE IT: BINOCULARS

Let's admit it, we've run through a few pairs of binoculars while seeking just the right ones — light enough to tote without getting an aching neck and of high enough quality to serve well without costing a fortune. (Prices begin at under $100 and proceed to the high hundreds or, for spotting scopes, the thousands.) We now have binoculars that suit us, but — and this is the point — *they might not suit everybody.*

To avoid the trial-and-error route, the best advice is to buy binoculars in person, if at all possible. Before buying, it's smart to question other birders; to study binocular evaluations, comparisons and advertisements in natural history and birding publications; and to check the editorial recommendations made by those publications and by such consumer-oriented magazines as *Consumer Reports.*

West, Southwest and Pacific Northwest, as well as western Canada and northward into Alaska; in the eastern half of the United States there's only one species, the ruby-throated. All hummingbirds are nectar-sippers, though not all come to feeders. Those species that do so are well worth courting with their favorite tipple of sugar water (page 99) and plantings of nectar-bearing flowers. Red, orange and pink blossoms are catnip to hummers.

JAYS. One or another of North America's eight jay species is to be found wherever a finger can point on the map. Jays are handsome and entertaining creatures, great favorites with most bird people and, presumably, with other bird species for which they serve as watchmen. (They give raucous alarm calls when a hawk, cat or any other menace is perceived.) Blue jays, scrub jays, Steller's, pinyon and gray jays are the best known of these near-omnivorous cousins of the CROWS and MAGPIES. *Peanuts (even in the shell), sunflower seed, cracked corn and other grain, mixed seed, safflower seed, peanut hearts, nutmeats, eggs, table scraps, suet and suet mixtures, baked goods, fruit.*

JUNCOS. Because of their varied colorings and markings, juncos once bore such specific names as white-winged, slate-colored, gray-headed and Oregon; these are now considered one species, the dark-eyed junco. (A field guide will help sort out the identity of local populations.) By whatever name, they're perhaps the most frequent visitors of all "feeder" birds, especially in severe weather; they're often affectionately called "snowbirds." *Millet, canary, niger (thistle), and other small seeds; fine-cracked corn, mixed seed, nutmeats, sunflower meats, peanut hearts,*

HUMMINGBIRD FLOWERS

See red (and pink and orange and yellow) when you choose flowering plants that will beckon hummingbirds to your place. Good bets: trumpet vine, shrubby and vining honeysuckles, monarda (bee balm), columbine, scarlet sage, red or rosy petunia and impatiens, and perennial phlox. To gild the lily, put a nectar feeder or two within or near a grouping of these plants.

*What! Is the jay
more precious
than the lark,
Because his feathers
are more
beautiful?*
—*Shakespeare*, The Taming of the Shrew, *Act IV*

suet or peanut-butter mixtures, baked goods.

KINGLETS, North American birds that belong to the family of Old World warblers and thrushes, are among the "maybe" feeder birds within their ranges. Both species, the ruby-crowned and golden-crowned, are known to sample foods from hanging feeders (preferred) or bird tables or trays, though they would rather feed on insects. *Suet and peanut-butter mixtures; also peanut hearts, nutmeats, baked goods.*

MAGPIES, black-billed or yellow-billed (the latter found only in California), are closely related to the CROWS. They fill the useful role of scavengers, feasting on such "found" treasures as meat, suet and table scraps; they are among the occasional surprise guests reported at feeding stations.

MARTINS (PURPLE MARTINS), which are swallows, live by catching flying insects; this makes them desirable backyard tenants wherever mosquitoes are a problem. Martins don't need our feeders, but they will eat eggshell bits and appreciate good housing for their sizable colonies. You can buy a martin "apartment house," or build one with the help of a how-to book.

MEADOWLARKS. These are open-country birds that nevertheless are learning to take the occasional feeder feast where they find it. The two species, eastern and western, fall into the large bird subfamily of New World blackbirds and orioles. *Grain, mixed seed.*

MOCKINGBIRDS (NORTHERN MOCKING-BIRDS), sweet singers not limited to the North by any means, love raisins that have been soaked in water. *Also: fresh fruit*

SINGING FOR THEIR SUPPER?

Well, no, they're not. Finding food and eating it keeps birds busy enough without performing dinner music at the same time. Male birds sing (and sometimes fight) to claim nesting territory by informing interlopers that the real estate is taken; and they sing (and sometimes fight) to attract a mate and possibly to maintain the bond between the pair. In some species, the "bond" song, if that is what it is, will be sung very quietly, *sotto voce,* by either parent while sitting on the nest. (In some species, notably the northern mockingbird, the females also sing.) Once the nesting season is under way, most singing will be at daybreak (the dawn chorus) and, less spectacularly, again at evening.

(especially citrus), suet or peanut-butter mixtures, peanut hearts, nutmeats, baked goods, hummingbird nectar.

NUTHATCHES. The four species of tree-climbing nuthatches all have backs of soft grey and either black or brown caps; they're longer-billed than the chickadees they somewhat resemble. White- and red-breasted nuthatches are the species most seen at feeders. Redbreasts prefer the coniferous forests of the North Woods and the West; the white-breasted species lives over most of the United States. *Suet and suet mixtures, sunflower meats and seed, peanuts, peanut hearts, melon seeds, nutmeats, baked goods; occasionally nectar from hummingbird feeders.*

ORIOLES. The orioles are among our brightest birds (so far as the males are concerned) and one of those fondest of fresh fruit and sugary solutions. The bird that was formerly called the Baltimore oriole is now the "northern." Many northern orioles now winter in their former summer range; the orchard orioles seldom stay past autumn. Other species: Scott's and hooded. Sugar water is the oriole's tipple of choice, but some birds visit other types of feeders. *Fruit (especially halved oranges), fruit jelly, suet, peanut-butter and suet mixtures, fine-cracked corn, millet, baked goods.*

PARAKEETS. Monk, green and canary-winged parakeets, either escapes or immigrants, are seen in the North as well as (more reasonably) Florida and southern California. They are said to be near-omnivorous at feeders, though we haven't yet seen feeder visits during the two summers we've glimpsed one or another of these exotics in our yard. *Seeds, grain,*

In winter, our resident birds often seem to sing just because it's a particularly sunny or mild day, perhaps in anticipation of spring. Migrating birds will sing during their long journeys.

Warning and "information" calls, as contrasted to birdsong, are ways to keep in touch with a mate or offspring or the rest of the flock, or to warn other birds of danger. Our resident jays used to keep track of our house cats (which are alas no more, after long lives) when they went strolling among the oak trees and rhododendrons — the squawks sounded just like *"Cat! Cat!"* as a posse of half a dozen birds turned the cats' casual gait into a sheepish slink toward home.

Other, quieter warning calls signal danger overhead from a bird of prey. These calls are said to be hard to hear — we've never picked one up. We know a hawk has passed over when birds vanish from the yard in a split second or (especially if they're downy woodpeckers) freeze in place. We'll keep listening, though.

baked goods, fruit; occasionally even suet.

PHEASANTS, more precisely ring-necked pheasants, have adapted well to semi-suburban as well as exurban and rural life. The brilliant gentleman and his harem of hens in their camouflage colors will peck up corn, other grain, or seeds quite comfortably while within a few yards of dwellings and can be counted on — the cock, at least — to greet the dawn with a peculiar barking call.

PIGEONS. *See* DOVES.

PINE SISKINS. A tiny species of finch, pine siskins travel and feed in flocks. They adore small seeds, including millet and niger (thistle) as well as sunflower seeds, but their tastes are not exclusive — they're also good customers for peanut hearts, nutmeats and suet mixtures.

PYRRHULOXIAS. *See* CARDINALS.

QUAIL, especially the northern bobwhites so familiar from the central United States to the East Coast and the California quail of the West, endear themselves wherever their quiet coveys come drifting from brushy cover to ground-offerings of grain or seeds. Not all quail (there are six North American species) will come to feeding stations, but many do. *Cracked corn, millet, sunflower seed, buckwheat, peanuts, peanut hearts.*

REDPOLLS, in some regions, are irregular visitors at best — in some winters they'll flock to feeders and any nearby wild foods after having been scarce or missing in their normal range in other years. There are two species, the common and hoary. *Niger (thistle) seed, sunflower meats,*

VANISHING ACT

It's July and suddenly the brilliant, squabbling mobs of goldfinches have disappeared from the thistle and sunflower feeders, where their presence has made up for the lack of other species that are now spread out to nesting sites. What accounts for the vanishing act?

Why, they're off to do their own nesting; their season is later than that of most other birds because they wait to reproduce until wildflower and weed seeds (their main natural foods) are ripening. (During nesting, however, they'll capture insects for their young, and they'll visit feeders occasionally, most often only one or two birds at a time.) After the brood is on the wing the adults will reappear in their usual flocks, bringing the new kids along to see where the host and hostess have put out the eats.

suet, suet mixtures, canary seed, bits of bread.

REDSTARTS. *See* WARBLERS.

REDWINGS. *See* BLACKBIRDS.

ROBINS. Of the three species found in North America, the American robin is the "redbreast" familiar from the edge of the Arctic to near the southern U.S. border. Robins will come for the drinking water (and the bathing) in a yard more often than for feeder victuals. They are most likely to come to feeders when they're migrating and very hungry, but we have smallish winter flocks, too, from time to time; they're good customers for the bird-bath even in icy weather. *Suet, suet mixtures, fresh fruit (especially apples, grapes and cherries), dried fruit (especially soaked raisins), peanuts and peanut hearts, nutmeats, baked goods.*

SISKINS. *See* PINE SISKINS.

SNOWBIRDS. *See* JUNCOS.

SNOW BUNTINGS. *See* BUNTINGS.

SPARROWS. The New World sparrows add up to about four dozen North American species. In addition, wherever humans live, there is also found the house sparrow (the so-called English sparrow), an introduced Old World weaver finch that thrives in cities almost without visible means of support. A field guide will help untangle the true sparrows likely to be seen at feeders during migration, off-season or nesting periods. The white-throated sparrow is a sweet singer and a busy rustler of leaves while seeking ground provisions; the song sparrow is also melodious. Other welcome yard species include the fox, chipping, field,

❝There is something distinctly human about the robin; his is the note of boyhood.❞
—John Burroughs' America

rufous-crowned, white-crowned and tree sparrows. *Various millets, sunflower seed and meats, fine-cracked corn, niger (thistle), canary seed, safflower, peanut hearts and peanuts, suet and suet mixtures, nutmeats, baked goods.*

STARLINGS (EUROPEAN STARLINGS), omnivorous in the wild, will gladly visit feeding stations for almost any food they can find, at any level. If they descend in flocks larger than you like to have around your feeders, you can lure them to another spot by putting down cracked corn, chick feed, reconstituted dry dog food and/or cooked rice or similar "cheap and filling" foods. *Also: seeds (especially millet), cracked corn, peanut hearts, peanuts, hulled oats, suet, fatty scraps or soft table leftovers.*

TANAGERS. Four of these brilliant subtropical species are known to breed in North America. The scarlet tanager, the best known, nests north of the mid-South; the reverse is true of the summer tanager. Other species are the western and the hepatic. Tanagers aren't easy to attract to feeders, but hosts they've favored with their company (not us) insist they can be lured by a mixed buffet. *Fresh and dried fruit, baked goods, suet mixtures, nutmeats, hummingbird nectar, sunflower meats.*

THRASHERS, like their cousins the CAT-BIRDS and MOCKINGBIRDS, are brush- or shrub-dwellers. Best known in the East are the brown thrashers, large, reddish ground-foragers with long, down-curved bills. The other thrasher species are the sage, long-billed, curve-billed, Le Conte's, crissal, California and Bendire's. Thrashers are sometimes willing to dine from low tables but prefer finding their feasts

TALKING BACK TO THE BIRDS

When we're outdoors and want to get a better look at the treetop creatures we can hear but can't see, there are some mouth sounds we make to tempt them closer for a better look and, perchance, for identification if they happen to be new to our ears.

Repeatedly making a kissing noise against the back of the hand, or producing an emphatic "spishing" sound with the lips, often brings curious birds

on the ground. *Fresh or dried fruit (especially soaked raisins), hummingbird nectar, scratch feed, sunflower meats and seed, cracked corn, nutmeats, suet mixtures, baked goods.*

THRUSHES. These members of the family of Old World warblers and thrushes aren't among the birds that spring to mind when feeder-frequenting kinds are listed, but some *do* patronize some offerings in some places, despite their natural shyness. Of the five regular brown thrush species, the hermit may stay through the winter; the wood, Swainson's and gray-cheeked thrushes may visit as they pass through as migrants. *Fruits (fresh or softened dried), sunflower meats, suet or peanut-butter mixtures, baked goods.*

TITMICE. The three North American titmice, tufted (mostly in the East), bridled and plain (mostly in the West), are closely related to CHICKADEES and are equally friendly feeders, relishing both fatty foods and seeds. The titmouse is acrobatic enough to peck suet (a favorite) from hanging feeders and versatile enough to sample offerings on the ground or a table. *Suet, suet or peanut-butter mixtures, baked goods (especially bread), shelled peanuts and peanut hearts, sunflower meats and seed, nutmeats, safflower, niger (thistle); occasionally hummingbird nectar.*

TOWHEES, five species, are among the New World sparrows. The rufous-sided towhee is most common; others are the California, canyon, green-tailed and Abert's. Towhees keep to low brush or shrubs and feed by vigorous foraging on the ground for seeds and insects — they scratch with both feet at once, in a sort of

close enough for the "spisher" (or "squeaker") to get a better look. If you can manage it, a vocal imitation of a particular bird's chortle, chirp or tweet can get a dialogue going, and sometimes the bird you're talking to will draw nearer to see who or what you are. Our red-bellied woodpeckers are willing interlocutors in this game, and chickadees enjoy chirping back to people very much indeed.

Finally, there's a little gadget called the Audubon Bird Call that can be manipulated to make various bird calls and songs, including a sound like that of a baby bird. It does indeed draw birds in the same fashion as the "spish," and it's fun to play with.

avian pounce that makes the leaves fly high. Though on the shy side, they do come to feeding areas, first looking on the ground but not disdaining bird tables or window shelves. *Millet, sunflower and mixed seed, niger (thistle), nutmeats, suet, suet mixtures, peanut meats and hearts, cracked corn, fruit.*

TUFTED TITMICE. *See* TITMICE.

TURKEYS, believe it or not, are occasionally reported as feeder visitors within their considerable range in the wild. (My favorite bird tale is of a particularly resourceful wild turkey who learned to use a hummingbird feeder.)

WARBLERS. Sorting out the dozens of species of birds that are *called* warblers — yellow warbler, prothonotary warbler, Tennessee warbler and many more — is a considerable undertaking. In the subfamily called wood warblers, there are many members that bear non-warbler names — examples are yellow-throats, chats, redstarts, ovenbirds, and parulas. Among the warblers some sojourning or migrating members will visit both hanging and fixed feeders; birdbaths and other sources of water are a great attraction. *Suet or peanut-butter mixtures, baked goods, crushed nutmeats, fine chick feed or fine-cracked corn, chopped fresh fruit or raisins, fruit jelly or preserves; occasionally hummingbird or oriole nectar.*

WAXWINGS. These birds aren't common at feeders, but both the cedar and Bohemian waxwings are known to appreciate halved or cut-up apples as well as raisins and currants (and a source of water)

❝*I am not . . . certain that I want to be able to identify all the warblers. There is a charm sometimes in not knowing what or who the singer is.***❞**
—*Donald Culross Peattie,* An Almanac for Moderns

when a flock makes one of its unpredictable appearances. On their own, waxwings subsist on wild and orchard fruits and berries plus airborne insects.

Myth 1

Squirrels That Put Their Minds to Raiding Feeders Can't Be Outwitted (or Hardly Ever)

Do we have to give up? *Facts:* The notion of squirrels' supremacy is partly true, alas. Some bird people never tire of trying to defeat the ingenious little beasties, perhaps mostly because they enjoy the battle of wits; such souls are the best customers for the innumerable "squirrel-proof" feeders on the market.

We consider our squirrel population a frisky part of nature's plan for the neighborhood and, in fact, we enjoy watching them outwit us almost as much as we enjoy trying ways to prevent them from eating too much of the birds' feast.

Strategies: Put squirrel food (corn, acorns, nuts) on the ground frequently and in generous quantities, placing it as far as possible from your feeding station. Or furnish other edible distractions — see "Corn on the Cob as a Squirrel Distraction" on page 109.

Put your sunflower meats and seed, which squirrels like a lot, into hanging or mounted feeders, not on the ground or on tables that squirrels can easily reach.

Gather and winter-store acorns and wild nuts (page 53) to put out as squirrel treats.

Use baffles (page 134) on the posts or stretched lines that support feeders, or hang feeders from tree branches on nonclimbable lines and beyond jumping distance from ground, trunk or limb.

Having done what you can, relax and enjoy the antics of this ingenious creature, which isn't going to wait for an invitation to share what we think of as *our* environment; here he comes, ready or not.

ON THE WATERFRONT

Waterfowl will often come ashore from both salt water and fresh water for offerings of food on the margin of an adjacent backyard. Mallards, black ducks and, for the lucky, wood ducks, as well as Canada geese and swans, will come to ground-scattered corn, wheat and other grains.

WOODPECKERS, a large tribe, include the resident birds that are most faithful to established food sources, so they're a special joy. The North American species list has 22 entries, including FLICKERS and sapsuckers. Among the many woodpeckers likely to visit feeders, besides the common flicker and yellow-bellied sapsucker, are the red-headed, acorn, downy (the No. 1 feeder customer among woodpeckers), hairy, pileated, three-toed and red-bellied. Woodpeckers are above all devoted to suet and suet mixtures, but one or another species will also take meat scraps, nut and sunflower meats, cracked corn, chick feed, even baked goods and raisins. (The red-bellied has the most cosmopolitan tastes, which go far beyond the usual woodpecker likings; it will also forage at ground level.) The best advice: start with suet, then add other offerings such as suet mixtures, and watch to see which are a success. *Good bets: sunflower seed, peanut hearts, shelled or unshelled peanuts, nutmeats; occasionally American cheese, fruit, hummingbird nectar.*

WRENS. Perkiness personified, these tiny birds include in their nine North American species the Carolina, cactus, marsh, sedge, house, Bewick's, winter, rock and canyon wrens. They aren't especially assiduous visitors at feeders anywhere, but some species, especially the Carolina and winter wrens (eastern U.S.) and the house wren (most of the U.S.) do visit occasionally. *Suet, suet mixtures, nutmeats, American cheese, baked goods, sunflower meats, peanut hearts, fresh fruit, hummingbird nectar.*

OUR BACKYARD — A HABITAT?

Even a few bird-friendly plants (for shelter, for food, for nesting) make any yard pleasanter for humans as well as birds, but the more plants the merrier, within reason. Most birds aren't attracted to overly dense growth — there must be openness and sunlight, too.

A survey of our informally planted place set among oak woods yielded this (partial) list of trees and shrubs that turns out to include many recommended for a planned bird habitat. There is oak, in plenty and in all sizes; wild cherry, tulip tree, shadblow (service-berry), witch hazel, sassafras, flowering dogwood, viburnum, dwarf pine, white pine, poplar, syca-more maple, black walnut, hemlock, cedar (juniper), rhododendron, azalea, yew, bar-berry, American and

When Found, Make a Note of . . .

C aptain Cuttle had the right idea in Dickens's *Dombey and Son* . . . whatever the fact that interests you, "when found, make a note of."

You can call your bird book a journal and keep it in chronological order through the months of each year, or just call it a notebook and organize it in the manner described below. Either way, you have a record of bird sightings and identifications and a place to compile lists and to note bits of behavior and, also, questions.

A setup that provides a generous number of pages for each month of the year suits us better than a straight year-by-year diary — it allows us to compare May of this year with May of last year or the year before without turning pages back and forth. About the middle of each month, we like to jot down an inventory of birds in residence, then note changes, or bits of behavior, or bright ideas about what we've observed.

For such a record you can use an attractive bound book with blank pages or, perhaps simpler, a loose-leaf notebook that is theoretically expansible forever. (Or purchase a copy of the Sierra Club's *Backyard Birder's Journal*, by Howard Blume, which has some helpful text as well as lots of space for notes and lists.)

Our own joint journal is kept near our best viewing windows, with binoculars and field guides at hand so we're ready to record the visit of anything short of a pterodactyl.

Japanese holly, boxwood, forsythia and euonymus.

There are (purposely) neglected corners where pokeweed, Virginia creeper and wild grapes grow unthreatened. Wild asters bloom here and there, where the grass is cut only once a season; there's even a clump of currants and gooseberries, plus a woodpile and a brush heap that birds like a lot.

In spots where there's enough sun, we grow a few herbs, vegetables and perennial flowers (including the gloriosa daisy, a favorite of birds). Ivy, myrtle and ajuga are the ground covers, and there is a partially shaded lawn made hospitable by the nearness of sheltering shrubs and trees.

If we had done more landscaping and done it with birds in mind, there would also be some shrub honeysuckles and trumpet vines for hummingbirds and more clearings for growing flowers, especially the nectar- and seed-bearers. But we'd hate to cut down more trees to get more sunshine, and the low-care landscape works just fine for the non-fanatical.

Our "Life List" of Yard Birds, So Far

In a raggedy way we've kept scribblings that add up to a pretty reliable list of the birds we've identified at our place so far; the modest total of species—55, as I write—seems to this pair of laid-back bird-spies to be surprisingly high for a handful of years on a wooded half-acre. The count grows by about 25 when we add species we've identified outside the yard. This "nearby" list doesn't include many abundant migrants, especially shorebirds and waterfowl, that we're still working on, field guides in hand.

All this counting has been done within a one-mile radius of our house, a fortunate circle that takes in a shallow, almost closed-off saltwater bay (locally dubbed a "creek"), a stretch of lively open bay extending to Long Island Sound in the distance, pebbly and sandy beaches, salt marshes and bordering woodlands.

The names used in the list below are those established by the American Ornithologists' Union.

Our Yard List

American crow
American goldfinch
American robin
Bald eagle (an
    immature stray)
Black-capped
    chickadee
Blue grosbeak
Blue jay
Brown creeper
Brown-headed
    cowbird

Brown thrasher
Canada goose
Carolina wren
Cedar waxwing
Common flicker
    (yellow-shafted)
Common grackle
Dark-eyed junco
Downy woodpecker
Eastern wood
    pewee
European starling

HELPING THE NEST-BUILDERS

Providing nest boxes and shelves is a whole subject apart that we can't get into here. However, birds continue to nest with or without birdhouses, as they've done for millennia, and as always they must scrounge far and wide for nesting materials.

To help with supply, we collect bits and pieces between nesting seasons. The lint removed from the clothes-dryer trap and the softener sheets used in the dryer go into a "recycle" box kept at hand; odd bits of white or pale-colored string

Evening grosbeak
Fox sparrow
Gray catbird
Great crested
  flycatcher
Green parakeet
Hairy woodpecker
Herring gull
House finch
House sparrow
House wren
Mourning dove
Northern bobwhite
Northern cardinal
Northern harrier
Northern mocking-
  bird
Northern oriole
Purple finch
Red-bellied wood-
  pecker
Red-breasted
  nuthatch
Red-headed wood-
  pecker
Red-shouldered
  hawk
Red-winged

blackbird
Ring-necked
  pheasant
  (including an
  albino female)
Rose-breasted
  grosbeak
Ruby-throated
  hummingbird
Rufous-sided
  towhee
Rusty blackbird
Screech owl (iden-
  tified by sound)
Sharp-shinned
  hawk
Song sparrow
Tufted titmouse
Whip-poor-will
  (identified by
  sound)
White-breasted
  nuthatch
White-crowned
  sparrow
White-throated
  sparrow
Winter wren

Additional Species Identified Not Far from Home

American
  woodcock
  (woods
  bordering creek
  marsh)
Bank swallow

(upland
  excavation in
  sandy soil)
Black-backed gull,
  lesser (bay,
  creek)

and yarn are put aside, together with soft cloth (like a worn-out pillowslip) that can be torn into strips. (String and strips of softener sheets and cloth should be cut into fairly short lengths, 6 to 8 inches.) Other things to keep in mind as nest-makings are feathers salvaged from an old pillow, facial tissues cut into ribbons, even combings from human heads and pet cats or dogs; if the cat, dog or human is a long-hair, so much the better. In horse-and-buggy days, some birds lined their nests with hair from Dobbin's mane.

When the birds start courting in spring, out go the nesting materials on conspicuous display. Put them in a basket (to prevent their blowing about) in an open spot near shelter, or stuff them into a mesh berry box or a temporarily surplus suet holder you can fasten to a tree or a post. Pile up some small twigs nearby, too, and add some straw, if you have it, and a large plastic plant saucer of mud (or a mud puddle) for the use of robins, phoebes and others that may need it for their style of construction.

Black-bellied plover (creek beach)
Black-crowned night heron (inland pond)
Black skimmer (bay)
Cliff swallow (creek and marsh)
Common loon (bay, creek)
Common tern (bay beach)
Ducks in great variety (bay, creek)
Great cormorant (bay)
Great egret (creek marsh)
Great horned owl (heard only)
Grebe, probably pied-billed (bay)

Gulls, assorted (bay, creek)
Hooded merganser (bay)
Horned lark (bay beach)
Least tern (bay beach)
Mute swan (bay, creek)
Osprey (creek and marsh)
Piping plover (bay beach)
Red-breasted merganser (bay)
Ruddy turnstone (bay and creek beaches)
Snowy egret (marsh)
Tundra swan (bay and creek)
Yellow warbler (marsh)

'Tis sweet to be awaken'd by the lark,
Or lull'd by falling waters; sweet the hum
Of bees, the voice of girls, the song of birds,
The lisp of children, and their earliest words.

—*Byron*, Don Juan, *Canto the First*

The Dining Area

◆

Your feeding station can be as simple as a windowsill tray supplied with seed from inside—a mini-station. Or it can be a whole outdoor environment designed for delight and dining—a maxi-station with birdbaths and/or drinking places, a ground-feeding area, one or two feeding tables, several post-mounted or hanging feeders, and plantings that are especially hospitable to birds.

Where there's little or no outdoor space: A window feeder, or a shelf built below a window or cantilevered on a porch or deck railing, will fetch visitors if it's kept supplied with mixed seed and an occasional extra (bread, cake, or pastry crumbs, birds' fruit salad, or suet mixtures). If you observe what seed is taken and what is left, you can switch to a different mix or, even better, buy the favored kinds separately and avoid waste.

A small yard: There's sure to be room for a bird table or a feeding shelf (post-mounted or fastened to a windowsill or ledge) and a birdbath, plus an area for scattering cracked corn or chick feed for ground-feeding birds. Add a post-mounted or hanging feeder for seed and another for suety foods, if you can.

A large yard: A mere feeding station can become a bird habitat extending right out to the edges of your property with a surprisingly small amount of effort but a

❝God gives every bird its food, but does not throw it into the nest.❞
—*J.G. Holland,* Gold Foil: Providence

bit more thought. There are excellent books on planting for the birds (check your library), and the National Wildlife Federation at 1400 16th St. NW, Washington, DC 20036, will send information on their official backyard habitat program. Local nurserymen can help you choose suitable plants.

Feeding on the Ground

Down-to-earth feeding is the first preference of scores of species, including many sparrows (tree, song, white-throated, white-crowned and chipping among them), cardinals, jays, doves, pigeons, towhees, thrashers, juncos, pheasants, quail, grackles and thrushes. Other species (chickadees, nuthatches) will eat on the ground by default if that's where the food is; even our family of red-bellied

---

Myth 2

Once You've Begun Winter Feeding, You Can't Interrupt It, Even Briefly

Must feeding be maintained without a break lest birds die for lack of the food you've been providing? (The "all or nothing" argument.) *Facts:* It's always preferable to keep feeders full, but as birds make the rounds of various food sources within their territory, they'll move on without more ado if a feeder doesn't pay off. They won't remember to check the same feeder forever if it stays empty, but if you can't find a stand-in you needn't feel guilty about being away for a few day. *Grain of Truth:* In severe weather many natural food sources and sources of water may be unavailable, and friendly feeding and unfrozen water can literally be lifesavers.

FLOCKING

Some resident birds tend to "flock" more than others in the off-season from nesting, either for purposes of defense from predators or for other reasons still being debated. The ones we're most apt to see in our area are the finches (including goldfinches), white-throated sparrows, mourning doves, and red-winged blackbirds and such flockmates as rusty blackbirds, grackles and cowbirds. Small not-quite-flocks — ornithologists call them "mixed flocks" — of winter birds move in on our feeders more or less in company several times a day. Chickadees, nuthatches, tufted tit-

woodpeckers will descend to earth on occasion, and so does the flicker. *The ground-feeding area* should be near sheltering shrubs or borders, but no closer than about 10 feet to protect against possible lurking felines. Not too much food should be put out at a time—a normal two days' worth is about right to avoid spoilage and waste. When more guests than usual fly in, however, you'll need to replenish the food more often.

Cleanliness counts. Rake up debris often: old, damp hulls, uneaten and perhaps decaying seed and grain, and assorted rubbish aren't healthful for the birds (and aren't too beautiful, either). As you rake, notice whether one or more kinds of food are being left uneaten; you may be spending money on a mixture that includes a seed or grain (buckwheat, for instance, at our place) that your visitors just don't go for. If that's the case, make your own mix (page 48) or switch to a mix with a different composition.

Just off the ground. A very low feeding table—6 to 12 inches above the ground, say—counts as a ground feeder, and so does a low stump, split logs laid flat side up, or a sheet of marine plywood laid flat. Food on such surfaces stays cleaner and drier than it would on the ground, and cleanup is easy. Birds that will dine at a slight elevation: some finches, sparrows, chickadees, jays, grackles, juncos, woodpeckers (downies, flickers, red-bellied, red-headed), cardinals, mockingbirds, nuthatches, tufted titmice, pine siskins, redwings, starlings, the occasional thrasher or thrush, and wrens.

Shelter. In snow country, a sheltered ground-feeding area (page 118) will be used gratefully by quail, pheasants, and many of the smaller birds, too.

mice and downy woodpeckers make up our "mixed flock," although members often appear on their own at other times. (In places favored by a high population of chickadees, titmice, cardinals and house sparrows, those birds will often form their own separate flocks, but we don't have that many.)

Our blue jays come in small groups, while crows are apt to show up in pairs. The bobwhites travel in sturdy groups of eight or ten, usually keeping close together and close to sheltering shrubs; robins seem to flock during migration and winter, which is when we see crowds of juncos, too. The ring-necked pheasant usually arrives alone for his corn ration, but he sometimes brings a second, younger male or his harem of two or three hens. When we spy a bright red male cardinal, we usually see his beautiful brown mate (with rosy bill) close at hand; no flocking for them. In fact, three or four birds are a whole college of cardinals for us.

So far, we've been spared any sizable groups of starlings, which can eat the cupboard bare very fast indeed.

The Feeding Table

Tables on the low side are most often recommended, although a table 3 feet high works fine as one of ours. (Also counting as tables are window or ledge shelves and platforms mounted as high as your hand can reach to fill them.) A good size is about 2 × 3 feet. If the top is solid, it needs corner drainage holes and/or a built-in tilt. An edge from a half-inch to an inch high keeps the food where it belongs and is appreciated by perching birds. We like our table with a windowscreen surface (page 125); it's easy to build and drains as fast as the rain falls. A no-carpentry table is a piece of plywood set on a stump; it can't get much simpler than that. A fancy touch would be ½-inch wood strips tacked around the edges as a wind baffle and spill-preventer.

Table diners include certain ground birds (cardinals, some sparrows, doves), but in our region they are mostly finches (including purple finches and goldfinches), chickadees, titmice, pine siskins, the occasional wren, jays, grosbeaks, redwings and other blackbirds, catbirds and mockingbirds (the last two will come for raisins or dried berries, preferably soaked until soft).

Table foods include fine-cracked corn (reserve coarse corn for the ground and for squirrels), sunflower seed and sunflower meats, peanut hearts (not for hot weather), mixed seed (again, observe to see which components are not popular), and the smaller seeds such as white millet and canary. The table is the place for certain treats: halved fruit or fruit salad; nutmeats; fruit jam or jelly; salvaged melon or squash seeds; Tabletop Suet, Corn & Nuts; crumbled bird breads and cakes;

THAT'S MY BILL . . .

Leisurely spying on visitors to your feeders (use binoculars for a spectacular increase in enjoyment) shows that seed-eating birds have stout, conical bills that help them deal with cracking and shelling large seeds as well as small kinds. You'll see this is true of cardinals, grosbeaks, juncos, and many birds whose names include "finch" or "sparrow." You'll further notice that being seed-eaters doesn't prevent many of the group from sampling suet and suet mixtures, fruit and other delicacies from time to time.

Tree-climbing birds, including creepers, nuthatches and the many, many woodpeckers, find

soaked raisins or other dried fruit; Kush-Kush Crumble; Bacon & Eggs. It's also the spot for table leftovers and for "test" foods the birds may or may not like, and for special foods for baby birds (page 87).

Hanging or Post-Mounted Feeders

Anything that can be fed in a commercial post-mounted feeder (there are many designs) could, in theory, be served in a free-hanging feeder if it weren't for the fact that some birds don't like to blow in the wind while they eat.

Post feeders are usually placed about head-high on a wooden or metal post that can be set permanently in place in the ground, inserted in a ground socket or mounted on a movable base. Some post setups will hold several feeders on their several arms.

Hanging feeders are dandy for tree-climbers or tree-clingers — chickadees, titmice and nuthatches enjoy swing-and-sway food even more than food that holds still — but because many birds won't eat from such lively devices it's not a bad idea to have both fixed and hanging feeders for both seed and suet. If hanging feeders only are deployed, they can be anchored by one means or another to permit only a little movement (page 133).

The birds to expect. On hanging or fixed seed feeders, chickadees, goldfinches (special thistle feeders are needed if you crave a lot of these), purple and house finches, titmice, grosbeaks, pine siskins, cardinals (on fixed feeders). On hanging suet feeders, woodpeckers (downy, red-bellied, red-headed), flickers, titmice, chickadees, nuthatches, yellow-breasted sapsuckers.

their food on tree trunks as they climb upward (or go downward, if they're nuthatches). The relatively slender, sharply pointed bills of the tree-clingers can probe into crevices and under loose flakes of bark for insects and larvae; if there are feeders nearby, the seeking bird may also encounter food stores stashed for future eating either by itself or by other birds — pantry robbery, so to speak. (Not just suet, but also acorns, seeds and grains are put away for a rainy day and, quite often, forgotten.)

Woodpeckers' bills are formidably backed by the pile-driving strength of neck and head that allows these birds to dig deeper than the smaller tree-clingers in search of food. Their bills also chisel out nest holes in dead trees and, in nesting season, drum often and loudly (on a tree, your house or a rain gutter) to assert their proprietorship over territory or to keep in touch with a mate.

Myth 3

Suet Isn't a Suitable Summer Food

Because it's a meaty item and summer is hot, the idea of suet raises doubts among beginners. *Facts:* Suet, which more or less corresponds to insects in the birds' diet, is a valuable source of energy at any time of year — woodpeckers dote on it year-round. In summer it's taken eagerly by parent birds, even those that are normally seed-eaters; they can feed babies better and faster this way, with less hunting around for the high-calorie diet the fledglings need.

Suet Strategy: Hang suet holders in the shade after May Day. Use only high-quality fresh suet, not bloody pieces, or use rendered suet, which keeps longer than fresh. (See "Suet Fresh & Rendered" on page 80.) If the climate is very hot and your suet tends to melt, you may want to bring the suet holder indoors during the midday hours. Replace summer suet after it has been outside for two or three days; change it sooner if you're in doubt about its freshness.

The foods to feed them. Niger (thistle) for goldfinches (and other finches, if the goldies will let them in) requires a tube feeder with tiny ports; it's well worth the investment (or nylon thistle-seed bags can be used). Put into hanging or post feeders any other kind of seed, especially sunflower, and nut or sunflower meats as a special treat, suet and suet mixtures or cakes (any of the solid "recipe" foods in this book), and occasionally an orange or apple half if you have no spike feeders for those.

Also in the hangable class are the Bird Feed Bag and the home-crafted milk-carton feeder, suet bell, stuffed pine cone, suet ball and grapevine wreath.

RESCUING A CAT-CAUGHT BIRD

It's a fact of life that pet cats allowed to go outside will catch the occasional bird despite all precautions, and another fact that they often see themselves as providers, not predators. In any case, they can't be blamed for doing what comes naturally. It's instinct to march proudly up to a human who works for them, holding a captured bird in mouth (or chipmunk, deer mouse, or some other four-footer); the message being delivered is "Look what I've brought for the family."

How to release the bird? Shrieks of dismay don't work — the cat will clamp down on the bird and/or run away. The best strategy is to heap verbal praise on such a wise, good, clever cat until finally, cross-eyed with bliss, the great hunter will allow itself to be stroked and petted. At that point, squeeze just under the cat's jaws with one hand and take the bird with the other when the jaws relax a little.

Tree-Trunk Feeders

Fixed "tree-trunk" feeders can perfectly well be mounted on the side of a stout post or even on a fence or the side of a building. They are meant for the tree-clinging and tree-climbing tribes, so naturally suet and suety foods are the ticket here. (See the recipes, and also the directions for devising various feeders beginning on page 117.)

The birds to expect: Look for delighted woodpeckers in variety (downies, hairies, flickers, red-bellied, red-headed), chickadees, nuthatches, titmice and, if you're lucky, the engaging little brown creeper. If you keep suet out in summer, many other birds that are nominal seed eaters will pay it a visit when they're feeding nestlings.

The hanging log (page 124) is not technically a tree trunk, but it's a great device for all the birds that will come to a fixed suet feeder.

Birds vs. Windows: Preventing Collisions

The sliding glass doors between our house and the deck, plus a bank of windows to one side, have been the scene of several bird crashes over the years. There has been only one fatality—a red-winged blackbird—but undoubtedly severe headaches have been felt by the other victims, including (twice) hawks in search of a meal.

The problem is a skylight that makes the interior as bright as outdoors at cer-

> Surprisingly often, a cat-caught bird that has been brought home to the family won't seem to be seriously injured. If it's dazed, keep it in a box under a towel until you see whether it can recover; if it's disposed to fly off immediately, let it go.

It's a warm wind,
the west wind,
full of birds'
cries;
I never hear the
west wind but
tears are in my
eyes.
For it comes from
the west lands,
the old brown
hills,
And April's in the
west wind, and
daffodils.
—*John Masefield, "The West Wind"*

tain times of day in spring, summer and fall, rendering the glass virtually invisible to birds. (The same effect can be produced by windows on two sides of a room.) Darkening our interior by lowering a blind over the skylight helps, and "flappers" applied to the glass doors provide added insurance. These work the same way as the silhouettes of hawks and owls that are sold for the purpose, but they may be more effective as visual alarms since they move with the slightest breeze.

For a simple flapper, cut a strip of cloth 18 inches long and 6 or 8 inches wide and scissor three-quarters of its length into narrow strips, leaving the top portion uncut; tape the top edge securely to the glass. (A small, fish-shaped kite or wind sock would work, too, and look quite decorative.) The idea is for the birds to see that there's something *there*, not just more outdoors. Flappers also work on windows that reflect the outdoors so faithfully that birds occasionally see an extension of the landscape and fly right into them.

FIRST AID

Birds aren't usually killed by window collisions (but it can happen). Put a stunned victim indoors in a box or basket, or even a deep pot, to recuperate; toss a towel over the top to prevent untimely escape. Sometimes an injured bird will be rarin' to go within minutes, but recovery can take hours, so be patient. In either case, the bird will let you know by its behavior when it's ready to be released.

What's Cooking?

Well, a whole banquet, if "cooking" can be taken to embrace all the bird foods you might possibly serve, most of which involve no cooking at all. From bird-food basics, the staff-of-life seeds and grains, we'll move on to more offbeat provender you can improvise, custom-cook, recycle or forage for (not necessarily in that order) and finally go to the recipe section. Birds' nutritional needs change when summer comes, so we've also discussed hot-weather food and its rationale.

Of the many kinds of seeds and grain eaten by feeder birds in America, some are "best bets" and some are not so popular. Both groups figure in our rundown of basics on page 50, drawn from a study by the National Wildlife Federation of the birds' own ratings of the most widely sold kinds of basic feed. Those birdy judgments may help you decide which kinds are most likely to be taken by your own backyard guests. You might try your hand, trial-and-error fashion, at mixing your own feed. No flat rules apply, so it's best to keep an open mind, observe what your birds eat and don't eat, and experiment. You'll soon discover the best balance for your backyard visitors.

As a further source of catering ideas, we've included a rundown of more than 100 possible food items beginning on page 54 — some of them perhaps surpris-

An enormous population of the migrants has been 'stopping over' . . . gathering, resting, feeding . . . they come, they go, they melt away, they gather again. . . . Some spirit of discipline and unity has passed over . . . waking in each flock a conscious sense of its collective self and giving each bird a sense of himself as a member of some migrant company.
—Henry Beston, The Outermost House

ing — with ways to use them for the benefit of the birds. Often overlooked possibilities include leftovers, recyclables from the kitchen (waste not, birds will want not), supermarket bargains, and wild foods (nuts, seeds, fruits, and so on). The recipes are from our kitchen notebook of how-to's for a range of easily made dishes — no-cook, barely cooked, briefly simmered, baked or rendered. Our guests find them alluring, and you can be sure they're nourishing supplements to yard birds' basic diet (which also includes what they glean for themselves in the neighborhood). The recipe section includes dealing with suet in its several forms and with supplying the summer nectar-sippers with their favorite tipple.

Once it's in full swing, a generous dining area that supplies seed/grain basics plus some of our recipe foods and miscellaneous "extras" has great value — perhaps at times even survival value — for the birds we all welcome as much for our own pleasure as for their benefit. Though statistics are still aborning, it seems likely that our human help will become increasingly important to backyard birds until some miracle reverses the rapid decline in habitat and degradation of environment going on everywhere. Until that over-the-rainbow day, our catering is one small step toward keeping these enchanting creatures among us.

*Behold the merry
  minstrels of the
  morn,
The swarming
  songsters of the
  careless grove.
Ten thousand
  throats that, from
  the flowering
  thorn,
Hymn their good
  God, and carol
  sweet of love.*
James Thomson, "The Castle
of Indolence"

Seeds & Grains, the Bird Food Basics

J ust about everything you need to know to get started with basic birdseed can be picked up in the next paragraphs. The list then comments on individual foods. *The first bag you buy.* Wild-bird food comes in various grades, some of which aren't easy to evaluate — they're all packed attractively and the small print (if any) isn't always helpful. You can buy from the supermarket, a garden center, a feed store or a bird-life specialist's shop or mail-order firm. (Mail order can be a boon; see the ads in birders' magazines.)

Price as an indicator. Read the price tag *and* the label. The best mixes will naturally cost more than lesser ones and will contain more sunflower seed or sunflower meats than any other single component. (This is why you check the label.

❝*You cannot catch old birds with chaff.***❞**
— *Proverb*

Myth 4

Raw Rice Kills

If fed raw, rice will swell in the birds' crops with harmful effects; therefore we shouldn't throw rice at weddings if there are bird bystanders near the church. *Facts:* This notion has been accepted so long . . . What's in it? Well, if rice is so bad, one ornithological wag points out, it will be news to the huge flocks of birds that descend on rice fields to feast in season. Case closed. However, birds that have a choice of foods don't pounce first upon either raw or cooked rice on the feeding table, although they'll eat it in a pinch, in which case cooked is more acceptable than raw.

Hulled sunflower costs more than whole seed, but there's no waste and it leaves no litter behind.) Be wary of a low, low price and of any label indicating the mix is bulked out with grains that many birds don't much like, such as wheat, oats, buckwheat and milo (sorghum).

Components. One good mix contains 30% sunflower meats plus white and golden millet, cracked corn and peanut hearts. Another good mix, this one intended for warm-weather feeding, drops peanuts and corn in favor of more sunflower and some canary seed.

Special mixes. For goldfinches (but also liked by other finches), finch mixes are a combination of niger (thistle) seed and chopped sunflower meats, or niger and canary.

Content check. If the mix proves to contain an undue proportion of twigs and pebbles and other inedibles, those are expensive ingredients.

Mixing your own. After watching "your" birds pick and choose among the ingredients of a purchased mix, you'll have an idea of which ingredients don't interest them. (But some of those might be eaten at another season or by other birds, which is why trial-and-error is the best way to go at first.) If small seeds such as millet and canary are going uneaten, buy "straight" black-oil sunflower seed and sunflower meats, fine-cracked corn and peanut hearts and stir up your own mix. Add some millet if you notice that seed has been taken fairly well; skip the millet if the birds are skipping it. Buy a bag of niger (thistle) for the finches and some safflower for the cardinals, both to be fed separately.

How much to buy. Especially in mild-climate areas, don't overstock; warmth

---

CLEANUPS: WHAT & HOW

Depending on how messy your birds are, plastic seed feeders need to be cleaned from a few times to many times a season, whenever they look clogged or cloudy. Dismantle the feeder if you can and scrub the parts with soap and water — a bottle brush helps. Be sure the feeder is thoroughly dry inside before it's refilled.

Nectar feeders for hummingbirds and orioles must be *kept* clean, not just cleaned occasionally (see page 101).

Birdbaths need frequent vigorous hosings if that's practicable, or at least a good scrub. Several refillings a day may be needed when business is brisk — the birdbath not only gets dust and grime from bathers, but birdbath litterbugs drop seeds and hulls into the water. (Why? Maybe the messy ones are trying to eat and drink at the same time.) In periods of little use, be sure to clean the birdbath

and humidity cause rapid deterioration of seeds and grains. A month's supply is about right, all things considered.

Storage. Securely covered trash cans are best. Even a thick plastic can may be gnawed open by squirrels and raccoons, so metal is recommended. To baffle those same beasts, use bungee cords to tie down the cover, or weight the cover with a plank and a concrete block or two.

At our place. We offer niger in cylinder feeders for the goldfinches; sunflower meats and black-oil sunflower seed separately in hanging cylinders for other off-the-ground seed-eaters; fine-cracked corn and a little sunflower and safflower seed (for the cardinals) on the ground; and, on the tables, a quick-mix of cracked corn,

often enough to prevent buildup of algae or slime.

Suet holders, feeders for bird cakes, and dishes for bird table foods need an occasional eyeballing and, if they don't pass inspection, a trip through the soapsuds.

Feeding tables need a hosing or a scrub occasionally if fruits and/or soft foods are put onto them directly. With any luck, rainfall will keep the table clean.

Areas for dining at ground-level, including the ground under hanging feeders, should be raked clean frequently for reasons of practicality (birds can't find food in deep litter and may even stop trying) as well as aesthetics and bird health.

Myth 5

Store-Bought Foods Containing Preservatives (or a Lot of Salt or Sugar) Are as Bad for Birds as They Are for Humans

In other words, would you feed a bird something you wouldn't give your family? *Facts:* Birds' digestions don't replicate humans', and there is no reason to believe that any food birds will accept is likely to hurt them. (In fact, birds like sweet and salty things and will even peck up salt "straight" -- and fat, also "straight," comes high on the menu of many species.) *Grain of Truth:* Food that is rotten or tainted *can* be harmful, depending on the organisms involved. Stay on the right side of doubt and never offer rancid, moldy or semi-decayed food of any sort, including seeds and grains that may not be in wholesome condition. (Reputable packers of birdseed and grain check their stocks for aflatoxin contamination, so that shouldn't be a concern.)

some millet, sunflower seed, sunflower meats, and a sprinkle of safflower. Other feeders around the yard, both hanging and fixed, hold special treats made from the recipes in this book. Miscellaneous additional eats — fruit, cheese, baby-bird food, melon seeds — go on the bird tables.

66*The songbirds might all have been brooded and hatched in the human heart.*99
—John Burroughs' America

Seeds & Grains & How They Rate

The numerical rankings in the list below come from a research study published by the National Wildlife Federation. The test was done to establish the degree of liking for 16 foods among 13 of the most common feeder birds. Minor foods (those with no ranking shown) and mixes weren't included in the study.

Barley (grain). Not a contender.

Buckwheat (grain). Often a filler; enjoyed by doves and cardinals.

Canary seed. No. 8. Not highly nutritious.

Chick feed or fine scratch feed (grain mixture for poultry). Dandy (get the fine-ground kind) for sparrows and other ground birds.

Corn (grain). No. 9. Most useful cracked (medium or fine); whole kernels can be managed only by the larger birds, from cardinals to pheasants. Jays will take dried corn from the cob.

Finch mix. Either niger (thistle) and canary, sometimes with some dwarf millet; or, preferably, niger and chopped sunflower meats.

Flax seed. Of limited interest.

Grit. Ground oyster shell can be added to your homemade wild-bird food; it's a poultry-feed item.

Hemp (seed). Once a standard food for cage and wild birds; now parched to prevent its sprouting into marijuana plants, so birds are said to like it less than they used to.

Myth 6

Peanut Butter, If Fed "Straight," Can Choke Birds to Death

Must peanut butter always be mixed with other foods? *Facts:* Ornithologists say that any dead bird found with peanut butter in its gullet has almost certainly died not because of its meal but because it was ill, or old, or freezing, or otherwise near the end of life when it took the mouthful. Those who are in doubt about peanut butter can mix in corn-meal before offering it, or include peanut butter in recipes (there are several in this book). Birds dearly love its taste, and it nourishes them well.

Millet (seed). Indispensable. White proso millet is No. 4; red proso millet, No. 6; golden (German or foxtail) millet, No. 7. If birds are ignoring the millet in a given mix, a switch to another variety may do it—there are many millets.

Milo (a kind of sorghum). No. 12. Can be a filler; moderately popular with doves and some other ground birds.

Niger (thistle) seed. No. 10. Loved by goldfinches and other finches. Needs special feeders since it's a tiny seed; popularly but inaccurately called "thistle."

Oats (hulled oats, or oat groats). No. 15. Some fans, but generally rates as a filler.

Peanuts and peanut hearts. Kernels are No. 5; peanut hearts (the "nub"), No. 11. Whole kernels should be chopped for all but blue jays.

Rape seed. No. 16. Nutritious but not much prized except by some finches and doves.

Rice. Will be eaten in a pinch by a few birds, including some sparrows and finches.

The north wind
doth blow,
And we shall have
snow,
And what will poor
Robin do then,
Poor thing?
He'll sit in a barn,
To keep himself
warm,
And hide his head
under his wing,
Poor thing.
—*Anonymous*

Safflower seed. No. 14. Cardinals love it; worth its high price if you want to attract more of them.

Scratch feed. See Chick feed.

Sunflower. The big one, sweeping the first three places. Black-oil (Perodovic) seed is No. 1; it's the most nutritious sunflower. Black-striped sunflower is No. 2. Hulled sunflower (sunflower meats or hearts) is No. 3.

Thistle seed. See Niger.

Wheat (grain). No. 13. Often a filler.

Beyond the Basics

In addition to the "recipe" foods in this book (and, of course, in addition to basic birdseed and grain), you can offer your bird guests small feasts based on recycled leftovers and other "kitchen" items, supermarket foods you may not think of as bird provender, and wild stuff that can be foraged in many areas of the country. The what's and how's of this offbeat tripartite catering are outlined in the chart that begins on page 54.

Recyclables: Leftovers, Trimmings & Other Throwaways

It's amusing (and money-saving too, which no one minds) to make good use of food you'd otherwise toss out. Some recyclables are fine as is; others are best in recipes, as indicated in the chart.

Before offering *any* food, however, you'll want to be sure it's wholesome in bird-diet terms. Soft, spotty or even half-rotted fruit, for example, is usually acceptable to birds — after all, they aren't choosy about the perfect stage of ripeness when they forage for themselves in an orchard or in the wild. But moldy, rancid, soured

66*You must not know too much, or be too precise and scientific, about birds and trees and flowers.***99**
—*Walt Whitman, "Birds"*

or decayed food is good for neither man nor bird, and in fact can cause illness. When in doubt, chuck any dubious item.

Market Buys

The chart lists items you can toss into your basket or cart along with "people" foods. Your fly-in guests will enjoy some of them "as is"; others are best used in recipes as indicated. Not-quite-pristine foods can be had for little or no money from the day-old-bakery-goods table, the butcher's suet bin, and the greengrocer's back room or "wilted" table.

One item sold at the market—bargain-priced bird food (page 47) —should *not* be bought there unless there's no alternative.

Foragers' Finds: Wild Stuff

Foraging for wild foods to serve to birds that visit your yard can be fully as satisfying as gathering nuts, berries, fruits, roots or greens to serve to your family (a considerable hobby with many). Although not everyone lives in an area overflowing with good wild foods, you'll find surprising riches in unlikely spots if you know how to look. Excellent foragers' guides exist for those who want to learn the what-where-when-and-whys of wild foods of all kinds. (Check your library or bookstore.)

Not all human-foraged foods may turn out to be popular with feeder birds. (However, some of your birds may be used to gleaning certain foods for themselves and will recognize them readily.) If you like the idea of rambling out to gather free food, any of your hauls are worth trying out, especially if your dining area is well established; birds used to good eatables seem more likely to try something unfamiliar. If a food is scorned, you've still had the pleasure of the search.

Go, from the creatures thy instruction take: Learn from the birds what food the thickets yield; Learn from the beasts the physic of the field . . .

—*Pope,* An Essay on Man, *Epistle II*

FOOD ITEM	RECYCLED	SUPERMARKET
ACORNS		
ALMONDS		Any kind, as a treat.
APPLES (SEE ALSO CRABAPPLES)	Spotty rejects; cores and seeds left from pie making.	All year.
BACON		For the fat (see Drippings) — you eat the bacon.
BANANAS	Overripe can be just right.	*
BARBERRIES		
BARGAINS		Soft or spotty fruit, marked down or discarded; "day-old" baked goods; suet or beef fat (may be free).
BAYBERRIES (WAX MYRTLE)		
BEECH NUTS		
BERRIES	Berries too soft for people are okay for birds, but don't use moldy ones.	Look for fading (but not moldy) berries in bargain-price baskets.

* Applies to obvious source.

FORAGED	SERVING AND/OR PREPARATION	STORING
Glean promptly in fall or squirrels will corner the crop.	Smash for bird table. To distract squirrels from feeders, toss whole onto ground far from dining area.	Spread out in cool, airy spot indoors.
	Crush or chop coarsely for bird table, or hang in fine mesh bag.	Freeze (preferable) or refrigerate.
Gather from old orchards in late summer and fall.	Halve whole apples and serve on spike (page 129) or bird table; put cores and scraps on table.	Refrigerate whole apples or trimmings (in baggie).
	Peel upper side; lay skin side down on bird table.	When fully ripe, refrigerate to prevent spoilage.
Fall and winter. The bushes are thorny— consider planting one or two so birds can pick their own.	Serve on bird table or ground.	Dry or freeze.
	Use fruit promptly. For fat, see page 80 or Meat Fat. Baked goods go on table, doughnut tree or spike (page 129).	Freeze fat or baked goods.
Gather from bushes, early fall. Yellow-rumped warblers are said to like them. If they fail to attract birds, use the wax to make colonial-style candles (but you'll need a *lot* of bayberries).	Try on bird table.	Spread out in cool, airy spot; use within a few weeks.
Glean these tiny nuts from the ground in fall, if you can get to them before the birds and squirrels. (Have a taste—they're delicious.)	On bird table.	Spread out in airy spot; use within week or two.
Summer and fall. See individual berries.	On bird table or ground.	Refrigerate to hold briefly; dry for future use.

FOOD ITEM	RECYCLED	SUPERMARKET
BISCUITS	Recycle as crumbs.	*
BLACKBERRIES		
BLACK WALNUTS		Shelled nuts are a specialty item.
BLUEBERRIES		Fresh or frozen, all year.
BONES	Both raw and cooked bones with meat attached.	Often can be had for nothing.
BREAD	Ends of loaves; crusts and scraps.	"Day-old" loaves, any kind.
BUTTERNUTS (WHITE WALNUTS)		
CAKE	Any kind, in bits and pieces.	Look for "day-old" bargains.
CAT FOOD		*
CEREAL, COOKED	Leftover oatmeal, farina, cornmeal mush, or other cereal, as is or in suety mixtures.	

*Applies to obvious source.

FORAGED	SERVING AND/OR PREPARATION	STORING
	Bird table or ground.	
These and related berries (dewberry, wineberry, raspberry, cloudberry, thimbleberry) ripen from early summer into fall.	Toss fresh or dried onto bird table.	To freeze, spread on baking sheet, freeze and tip into freezer bags. To dry, use warm oven, sunlight or food dehydrator; store in airtight container.
Early fall; from ground.	Husk and spread in airy indoor spot to cure for 2–4 weeks. Smash rock-hard shells and spread nuts on bird table or ground; let birds pick out meats.	Store whole nuts in cool, airy spot; freeze if shelled.
Summer into early fall. Low- and highbush sorts; also huckleberries (the ones with seeds).	Serve as is, on bird table or ground.	Freeze or dry any surplus (see Blackberries).
	Hang in shady spot for tree-climbing birds.	Wrap and refrigerate for a week or two, or freeze up to a month.
	Chop or crumble for bird table; use in recipes. (White bread is the prime attention-getter for a new dining setup.)	Bag and freeze indefinitely.
Rare, but worth seeking; early fall.	See Black Walnuts.	See Black Walnuts.
	Crumble for bird table.	Bag and freeze up to 2 months.
	Put a saucer of high-quality canned cat food on bird table, or include in suety mixture to add protein.	
	Mash and put out in dish on bird table (good for babies in nesting season, too); use in recipes.	Refrigerate several days, or freeze up to 2 months.

FOOD ITEM	RECYCLED	SUPERMARKET
CEREAL, READY-TO-EAT	Bottom-of-the box remainders.	*
CHEESE, AMERICAN TYPE	Leftover bits and pieces.	*
CHERRIES		
CHESTNUTS AND CHINQUAPINS		
COCONUT	Scraps and parings of fresh, remnants of packaged.	*
COOKIES	Scraps and crumbs.	*
CORN BREAD AND CORN MUFFINS	Leftover chunks and crumbs.	
CORNMEAL		The yellow, more nourishing kind is preferable for birds.
CORN ON THE COB, FRESH OR FROZEN	*	*

*Applies to obvious source.

FORAGED	SERVING AND/OR PREPARATION	STORING
	Crumble for bird table; use in recipes.	Store in airtight container.
	Spike in holder (page 129), hang chunks in Bird Feed Bag, or grate coarsely for table. Before using, trim off any mold.	Refrigerate or freeze.
Black cherries or chokecherries are worth bringing home for birds in summer (or for preserving pan).	Serve as is on bird table.	Refrigerate a few days; freeze up to 2 months.
Native chestnuts have been blighted out of our forests, but imported strains are now planted for orchards and landscaping. Southern foragers might find chinquapins, with rather perishable nuts.	Serve as is on bird table or ground.	Freeze if not used promptly.
	Chop for bird table or serve in shell (page 82); use in recipes.	Bag and freeze.
	Sprinkle crumbs on bird table or use in recipes.	Keep in airtight container.
	Chunks in Bird Feed Bag; crumbs on bird table or for recipes.	Refrigerate several days; freeze up to 2 months.
	Use in recipes.	Keep in airtight container at room temperature, or refrigerate or freeze.
	Tack up an ear for the jays, or cut off the kernels and scatter on table or ground.	Refrigerate 2–3 days.

FOOD ITEM	RECYCLED	SUPERMARKET
CRABAPPLES		
CRACKERS	Save bottom-of-the-box scraps to make crumbs.	*
CRANBERRIES		
CRUMBS	Save any non-gooey baked goods: bread, cake, dry cereal, crackers, biscuits, corn bread, potato chips muffins, pancakes, pretzels, toast, pastry without icing or filling, doughnuts, waffles, cookies.	Day-old baked goods are often bargains.
CURRANTS, DRIED		*
CURRANTS, FRESH		
DOG FOOD		*
DOUGHNUTS	Slightly stale doesn't matter.	*
DRIED FRUIT	Odds and ends, even if very dry.	Currants, prunes, raisins and other kinds.

*Applies to obvious source.

FORAGED	SERVING AND/OR PREPARATION	STORING
From home landscaping or abandoned plantings; early fall.	Cut open to expose seeds; put on bird table.	Refrigerate up to 2 weeks; still okay for birds if soft or spotty.
	Crumble for bird table or for recipes.	
Found wild in fall in fortunate regions.	Chop slightly or serve whole. Set out on bird table or string into garlands for holidays (page 131).	Freeze indefinitely.
	A food processor makes crumbs fast. Serve on bird table or ground; use in recipes.	Save dry crumbs in airtight container; if moist, store in freezer.
	Use as substitute for raisins in recipes, or soak until plump and serve on bird table.	Store in airtight container.
Uncommon, but they exist.	Use in fruit salad (page 95) or "as is" on bird table.	Refrigerate a few days, freeze, or dry in food dehydrator.
	Dried puppy biscuits are great in recipes or, when crushed, for the bird table. Canned dog food is enjoyed "straight" (in a little dish on the table) by many birds; it's also valuable for increasing protein in suety mixtures.	
	Spike on holder (page 129) or twig, drop into Bird Feed Bag or suet holder, or make crumbs for table.	Refrigerate a few days, or freeze indefinitely.
	Soak, chop and serve in dish on bird table. Serve stewed dried fruit the same way.	Store dry fruit in airtight container; refrigerate soaked or cooked fruit 3–4 days.

FOOD ITEM	RECYCLED	SUPERMARKET
DRIPPINGS	From roast beef, pork, lamb, veal, poultry or ham, bacon or plain-cooked meat dishes.	
EGGS (INCLUDING DRIED EGGS)	Leftover scrambled eggs, omelets, hard-cooked or poached eggs.	*
EGGSHELLS		*
ELDERBERRIES		
FAT: SEE DRIPPINGS; MEAT FAT; OIL; SUET (PAGE 80)		
FISH	Fish in a dish doesn't sound like an avian item, but you can never tell — and cooked scraps are a good source of protein.	
FLOUR		For recipes, especially as a binder of "loose" fatty mixtures.
FRENCH TOAST	*	
FRUIT (SEE ALSO INDIVIDUAL FRUITS)		*
GOOSEBERRIES		
GRAPEFRUIT	Shells left from breakfast make dandy bowls for cut-up fruits or fruit salad (page 95). Bag and refrigerate up to 5 days.	*

* Applies to obvious source.

FORAGED	SERVING AND/OR PREPARATION	STORING
	If moisture remains, simmer drippings until it evaporates (bubbling will stop). Strain into jar. Use in recipes.	Refrigerate a few weeks or freeze indefinitely.
	Set out in dish on bird table.	Refrigerate a day or two.
	Rinse out, air-dry, crush. Offer "straight" on bird table or ground as source of calcium and grit, or include in recipes.	Cover and keep at room temperature.
Gather in late summer.	Serve as is on bird table, or dry in warm oven, sunlight or food dehydrator.	Refrigerate fresh a few days; if dried, store in airtight container.
	Set out on bird table.	
	Chop and scatter on bird table.	Refrigerate 2–3 days.
	Cut up into bowl (or citrus shell) for bird table; or mix together to make fruit salad (page 95), serving all the juice.	
Plant-escapes from gardens are sometimes found in midsummer (few gardeners grow these now).	If large, squash or chop before offering on bird table.	Drying to keep for future use should be feasible.
If you live where this citrus grows, there may be an abandoned grapefruit tree to winter-forage from.	Grapefruit flesh, though not a bird favorite, can be included in fruit mixtures.	

FOOD ITEM	RECYCLED	SUPERMARKET
GRAPES	Soft or half-spoiled specimens look just fine to birds.	*
HAMBURGER	An ideal use for the surplus when you've bought a little too much.	*
HAWTHORN FRUITS		
HAZELNUTS (FILBERTS)		*
HICKORY NUTS		
HONEY		*A caution:* Honey is included here because it is *not* good for birds in general (especially nectar-eaters) unless the feeding is expertly managed to avoid health risks. Use sugar instead.
HUCKLEBERRIES		
JAM, JELLY	*	*

*Applies to obvious source.

FORAGED	SERVING AND/OR PREPARATION	STORING
The favorite of autumn foragers, both human and winged. Grapes occur in great variety and grow almost everywhere. If you pick some for jelly, share them with your outdoor guests.	Put on bird table, either whole or squashed a little to make them easier to eat.	If still firm, refrigerate for a few days; otherwise, serve at once.
	Serve raw or cooked and crumbled on the bird table, or use in recipes.	Fresh meat is preferable; freeze if it must be kept.
Shrubs are too thorny to afford easy picking of their autumn fruits (haws), but berries are good candidates for a self-service bird banquet. (Wear stout gloves if you go out a-picking.)		
Gather in fall.	Remove husks. Crack and serve, shells and all, on bird table or ground.	Refrigerate or freeze.
All hickories (shellbarks or shagbarks, mockernuts, pignuts) are loved by squirrels and by any birds that can get at the meats. If you snaffle some in fall, spread them out to cure awhile in an airy spot.	Crack or slightly smash shells; put on bird table or ground.	Store in a cool, airy place.
These are the little "blueberries" with seeds. Gather from midsummer into fall. See Blueberries.		
	Fruit preserves are highly popular with sweet-loving birds (the species that will pilfer the hummingbirds' nectar, for instance). Put an occasional saucerful on the bird table.	

FOOD ITEM	RECYCLED	SUPERMARKET
LARD		Can replace rendered suet or other fat in recipes.
MEAT FAT	Clean trimmings from cooked/uncooked beef; firm, fresh fat from other meats.	*
MEAT SCRAPS, FRESH	*	*
MELONS (SEE ALSO MELON SEEDS)	Leftover flesh from family portions.	*
MELON SEEDS	Avidly taken by birds (as are seeds of winter squash and pumpkins).	
MILK, LIQUID OR DRIED		*
MOLASSES		*
MOUNTAIN ASH (ROWAN) **BERRIES**		
MUFFINS (ANY KIND)	*	*
MULBERRIES		
NUTS: (SEE ALSO INDIVIDUAL NUTS)		*

* Applies to obvious source.

FORAGED	SERVING AND/OR PREPARATION	STORING
	Render fat (page 80) and use in recipes, or offer in suet feeder (page 123).	Refrigerate 1–2 days; freeze up to 2 months.
	Use in recipes (Crackling Cakes, Meatballs from Bits & Pieces, etc.).	Freeze up to a month.
	Use in fruit salad (page 95) or serve as is on bird table.	
	Rinse free of pulp and membrane and serve on bird table. Air- or low-oven-dried seeds can be ground and used in recipes.	Bag and store dried seeds at room temperature 1–2 weeks, or freeze up to 3 months.
	For recipes, or for soaking bread and serving to parents that are feeding nestlings.	
	Use in recipes.	
The heavily berried tree may be a street planting or a wilding; gather berries in autumn.	Serve as a bird-table offering.	Store surplus in freezer
	Hang out in Bird Feed Bag, crumb for bird table or use in recipes.	Refrigerate for a few days, or freeze.
Summer fruits, found on (or under) big, messy mulberry trees.	Serve as is, or include in fruit salad (page 95).	Refrigerate a day or two; to keep, freeze or dry as described under Blackberries.
Good nut years yield bigger fall crops than squirrels can deal with all at once; get out there fast and you'll stand an excellent chance against the competition.	Birds will do the picking if you smash the shells and put the whole business on the bird table or the ground. Whole nuts thrown at a distance from the dining area may help distract squirrels from the birds' portion.	Store in coolest possible place—freezer is ideal.

FOOD ITEM	RECYCLED	SUPERMARKET
OIL, COOKING	Salvaged as "drippings," any clean oil *that isn't highly seasoned* is fine in recipes for bird breads and such as well as for enriching mixtures that need more calories.	*
ORANGES		*
PANCAKES		
PEANUT BUTTER	Never waste a smidgen.	*
PEANUTS, ANY KIND	The last few in the jar will be welcome, even if (mildly) seasoned and salted. Birds like salt but not peppery tastes, so exotic nuts should be rinsed if you're in doubt.	*
PEARS		*
PECANS, PECAN MEAL		*
PIE CRUST	Bake leftovers of pie dough instead of pitching them out.	

*Applies to obvious source.

FORAGED	SERVING AND/OR PREPARATION	STORING
		Refrigerate.
If there's an unclaimed orange tree in your neighborhood, investigate for possible fruit; birds don't care if oranges are ugly.	Halve and spike on a holder (page 129) as special treat for orioles and finches. (If squirrels can reach the fruit they, too, will nibble.) Include in fruit salad (page 95).	Fruit will keep in cool place at least 10 days.
	Dice or crumble. Strew on bird table, or use in recipes.	Refrigerate a few days, or freeze.
	Blend with cornmeal and scatter as crumbs on bird table, or use in recipes.	Store in cupboard.
	Serve on bird table or ground or hang in mesh bag; use in recipes.	Store in cupboard.
Keep an eye out for old trees, which can bear even when neglected; if you see snowy blossoms in spring, follow up in autumn.	Just before serving, halve whole pears and spike on holder (page 129). Set out on bird table; put cores and scraps on table.	Refrigerate as soon as fruit is ripe (feel base of stem for yielding), as it spoils quickly.
Where pecan trees flourish, these rich nuts can be gathered with some ease. Birds love them; pecan meal (available by mail from southern nut merchants) is good as is on the bird table and in recipes.	Crack shells and spread nuts on bird table or ground; let birds pick out meats.	
	Crumble for bird table.	Keeps at room temperature (or refrigerated) up to a few days after baking.

FOOD ITEM	RECYCLED	SUPERMARKET
POPCORN		*
POTATO CHIPS	Save broken bits and pieces; birds love their saltiness, which does no harm (and salt may be a necessity).	*
PRUNES	Fruit that has dried up in the box or is left over after stewing is acceptable.	*
PUMPKIN SEEDS: SEE MELON SEEDS		
RAISINS	Dried out or not, remnants from the raisin box are loved by catbirds, mockingbirds and robins if they're soaked to plump them up.	*
RASPBERRIES: SEE BLACKBERRIES		
RICE	Not high on the list of favorites, but some species like it. Leftover cooked brown or white rice is more acceptable than raw.	*
SALT, COARSE		*
SHORTENING, VEGETABLE		*

*Applies to obvious source.

FORAGED	SERVING AND/OR PREPARATION	STORING
	String garlands of plain or buttered popcorn for winter trees or birds' Christmas tree (page 111); use in recipe for Nutty Popcorn Balls (page 103) and hang in Bird Feed Bag or crumble for table.	Store airtight at room temperature up to 2 weeks.
	Crush for bird table.	Will keep in airtight container 2 weeks or more.
	Slice or chop dried fruit for manageability; cut up soaked or stewed fruit. Serve in dish on bird table.	Store dried fruit in cupboard; refrigerate if cooked.
	Put soaked raisins in dishes on bird table; for recipes, use straight from box.	
	Scatter on bird table.	Refrigerate for a few days; freeze up to 2 months.
	Birds often crave salt; put out a shallow dish near other food on table or ground.	
	Can replace suet, drippings or lard in recipes.	

FOOD ITEM	RECYCLED	SUPERMARKET
SOYBEANS		*
SQUASH SEEDS: SEE MELON SEEDS		
SUET: SEE PAGE 80		
SUGAR AND OTHER SWEETENERS (EXCEPT HONEY)		*
SUNFLOWER SEEDS		
SYRUPS	Use what's left in maple- or corn-syrup bottle.	*
TABLE SCRAPS	*	
WAFFLES (WITHOUT SYRUP)	*	
WALNUTS		*
WHEAT GERM		*

*Applies to obvious source.

FORAGED	SERVING AND/OR PREPARATION	STORING
	Cook until very soft and offer on table for birds that are feeding their young.	
	Use in recipes or as main ingredient of nectar for hummingbirds and orioles (page 99). Some birds take sugar "straight" from a dish.	
On summer or early fall rambles, keep an eye out for roadside sunflowers heavy with seed, a treasure. When seeds are ripe, take home whole flower heads and let them dry out.	Tack whole flower head to side of house, fence or post; birds will help themselves. Or rake out seeds for feeder or bird table.	Keep cool and dry and away from mice and squirrels.
	Dilute leftover syrup with equal portion of water, and hang out in a vial or cup where sweet-loving birds can dip a bill. (For systematic feeding of hummingbirds and orioles, see page 99.)	
	Run a test or two with likely foods, setting them out on bird table. (I've read of birds that like kippered herring, so there's no telling what might ring the bell.)	
	Dice or crumb for recipes or bird table.	Refrigerate a few days, or freeze up to 2 months.
Can sometimes be foraged.	See Black Walnuts.	See Black Walnuts.
	Adds good nutrients to recipes.	

Recipes (Really) for the Birds

The idea here is to get into and out of the kitchen swiftly, bringing with you, as you emerge, a nutritious and delicious special treat for your "freeloaders" with wings. Some of our recipes involve no cooking; others require very brief labor over a hot stove; still others, such as rendering a good big supply of pure suet for little or no money, take some time but no real work. Bakers will like the breads and cakes, and so will the birds. Our recipes aren't written in stone, as you'll see from the many suggestions for variations, and bird-hosts worth their kitchen salt will feel free to devise still other versions.

The how-to-serve information in each recipe is a clue to which group(s) of birds will most welcome the food when it's offered in the suggested fashion. You can also look into specific birds' dining preferences on pages 17–32.

For our purposes, birds can be grouped in a general way by their favored manner of feeding — on the ground, on a table or shelf, on a tree trunk, or from hanging feeders — although they'll switch when necessity compels or the food looks better over there than here. Thus, if a recipe says the food should be strewn on the bird table and ground, you'll know it's not for woodpeckers or other tree-clingers but for doves, sparrows, juncos, cardinals, blackbirds, and so on through the list of down-to-earth species, plus the table diners — the great middling class of mainly seed-eating birds that nosh a little here, a little there, but generally favor a level playing field and don't much like midair food sources. Many ground birds will ascend

WHO EATS FIRST & OTHER RULES OF THE FLOCK

"Pecking order" involves more hierarchical bluff and bluster than physical attack. You'll notice that some birds of a species wait while others feed, obeying an order of precedence evidently based on the sex, age and pugnacity of individual members of the flock. The birds waiting in a bush while the first-comers gorge will be the same individuals each time. The top bird, a male, knows who's the boss of bosses, and so does the flock.

When various kinds of birds find themselves together, some seem naturally timid. Our brown

to the table for a mouthful, and some versatile hanging-feeder types (chickadees, nuthatches, finches and titmice) will fly in for a table landing. Even woodpeckers, especially flickers and red-bellies, will occasionally hop out of the woods into a ground dining area or onto the table for a change of menu.

Similarly, one of the baked or suety foods, when hung out in your Bird Feed Bag or other free-swinging feeder, is meant for chickadees, nuthatches, finches and titmice, which positively enjoy a swinging feeder but will visit fixed ones too, and not for cardinals or other birds that hate to be buffeted by the wind as they dine. The large woodpeckers and the brown creepers prefer their food firmly attached to a tree trunk or post, not swaying in the breeze, but small woodpeckers (downies and hairies) as well as the aforementioned "swingers" will take suitable (suety) food in either setting; so will the Carolina wrens who live at our place and seem to sample foods of many kinds at every level.

creeper, for example, never challenges a downy woodpecker, a nuthatch or a titmouse that has gotten to a suet tree first. The downy retreats when the red-bellied woodpecker appears; the hairy woodpecker doesn't come when any other bird is in sight, as far as we can tell; and a single house finch can always chase a chickadee or a tufted titmouse away from the window feeders.

Serving It Forth

Many of our recipe foods can be served in more than one way and thus to more than one group of birds, if they're following their usual preferences in feeding locales. Chunks or muffins, for example, might be served in a cake basket or suet feeder, hung in your Bird Feed Bag, chopped for the bird table, packed into a milk-carton feeder for hanging, plastered over a wire or grapevine base, or put into holes drilled in a feeder log. Other dishes, such as Kush-Kush Crumble, are meant for one style of feeding (the table, in this case) or for only one or two ways.

Among the recipes to choose from according to season (seasons are indicated with each recipe) are fruity suet puddings, some baked breads and cakes, a stovetop cornmeal and bacon-fat pone, and an array of suet cakes both pristine and enriched with cracklings, fruit, seed, nuts, coconut, or high-quality dog food. There are also some crumbly meals and mixes, a granola concoction, and some other things our own fly-in guests like a lot. For more food ideas, see pages 54–73 for a charted rundown of bird-food possibilities.

I sing of brooks, of blossoms, birds, and bowers,
Of April, May, of June, and July flowers.
— *Robert Herrick, "The Argument of His Book"*

Myth 7

Summer Feeding Isn't Such a Good Idea

Is summer feeding unnecessary and a waste of time? *Facts:* Offering summer food is rewarding to humans *and* most helpful to birds, especially when they're raising nestlings and most especially in semi-citified areas where natural food sources are declining. (One ornithologist has tabulated almost a hundred species that patronize summer feeders — suet, alone, is taken by some 80 species.) *Grain of Truth:* Natural foods *are* more plentiful in summer, and birds can certainly get by without help, but they do better (and are closer at hand for you to enjoy) when you lend a hand. Summer feeding prompts parent birds to bring the newly fledged chicks to see where the good stuff comes from and encourages the year-round species (and their children) to keep our place in mind when summer's over and the pickings are slimmer elsewhere. *Summer Strategy:* Keep only a few feeders going in summer, not a full winter quota (see page 84). Clean and plentiful water is of first importance, as always. *Baby Food:* For parents to take to babies in the nest, put out some of the soft foods suggested on page 87.

Apple Pudding

SEASON: Cool or cold weather, but acceptable all year.

FEEDER: Bag, cake basket or suet holder, can/pans, suet bell.

METHOD & TIME: No cooking (except to warm fat); 10 to 15 minutes.

YIELD: About 2¼ pounds.

Appealing because it's fruity and sweet, this no-cook mixture is also rich in the fat that birds appreciate and require year round. (Whenever a new batch is put out, it starts a virtual feeding frenzy among our woodpeckers, titmice and chickadees.)

A food processor, though not essential, makes short work of creating crumbs and chopping apples.

◆

2 cups rendered suet (page 80), bacon fat or lard
3 cups chopped apples, including cores and seeds
1 cup brown sugar, packed
1 cup chopped raisins
3 cups dry crumbs (bread, cake or cookie)
1 cup rolled oats (any kind)
1 cup peanut butter (any kind)

◆

In a skillet or saucepan, warm the fat just until pourable. Meanwhile, stir together the remaining ingredients. Gradually add the fat to the fruit mixture until a sample just holds its shape when squeezed. (Save any surplus fat.)

Press into muffin cups fitted with

"PIES" IN DISPOSABLE PANS . . .

Press any of the suet cake or pudding mixes into individual foil pie pans, packing the food in well. Optionally, stretch a piece of onion bagging over the face of the "pie" and pin it together at the back of the pan. To feed, tack the pie to a post or a tree, using two or three nails to keep it from revolving (or tearing loose) when birds make a landing.

. . . AND CANS

Clean tuna or cat food cans may be used in the same way as disposable pie pans, above.

Foil pans are refillable right in place.

paper liners, or pack into a loaf pan or square baking pan lined with plastic or foil. Clean tuna or cat-food cans can also be used (no need for liners). Chill until firm.

Another shape: The mixture can be shaped into a suet bell (page 127) to make an attractive Christmas or anytime gift for a bird-feeding friend.

To serve: Hang one or two "muffins" (without their paper liners) or a hefty chunk in your Bird Feed Bag, or put into a suet holder. Tack filled cans to a post or tree. Hang suet bell.

To store: Refrigerate, wrapped, up to 3 days, or freeze up to a month.

Bacon & Eggs

SEASON: Year round.

FEEDER: Bag, cake basket or suet holder, bird table.

METHOD & TIME: Stovetop or oven; 15 to 20 minutes.

YIELD: 6 cupcakes or 1 skillet cake.

The high-protein/high-calorie combination of bacon fat and eggs is one to bear in mind while parents are feeding insatiable young. It's also one to remember if you should ever have to rear an orphaned nestling yourself.

◆

⅓ cup bacon drippings
6 eggs, beaten

◆

Warm the bacon fat in an 8-inch skillet. Add the fat to the beaten eggs; mix well.

GOOD TASTE & MENU ODDITIES

Any doubt that birds have a sense of taste (and some peculiar tastes) is dispelled when highly seasoned fat is offered to a fat-loving set of birds. They just won't go for such recyclings as the rich skimmings of herbed and garlicked stew or the floating fat from a pot of chili, so it's useless to use such fats in bird recipes as you would the blander drippings of bacon, beef or ham.

Such a dislike, though, is less striking than certain

To cook as an egg cake: Return the mixture to the skillet; cook over very low heat, covered, about 10 minutes or until firm.

To make "cupcakes": Preheat the oven to 300°F. Pour mixture into 6 nonstick muffin cups (or regular muffin cups with paper liners); bake about 15 minutes or until firm. Let cool.

To serve: Hang (peeled) cupcakes or a chunk in your Bird Feed Bag, or put into a suet holder. Chop coarsely for the feeding table.

To store: Refrigerate, wrapped, up to a week.

RECYCLED LEFTOVERS. Uneaten hard-cooked, scrambled or fried eggs needn't be tossed. Just chop and serve in a saucer on the feeding table in any season.

Leftover egg yolks, often in surplus in households concerned about cholesterol, can be served to birds with no health worries. Use yolks in place of whole eggs to prepare Bacon & Eggs (above), or prepare chopped or mashed yolk — an especially fine food for parents to take to the nest and also for the orphaned nestling.

To cook the yolks drop them whole, one at a time, into simmering water and poach about 5 minutes or until firm. If yolks aren't intact, stir and poach in a custard cup set in simmering water. Let cool, then chop or mash.

Microwave: Stir up to 3 yolks together with a fork in an oiled 1-cup measure (1 or 2 yolks can be done in a custard cup). Cover with waxed paper, and microwave on medium power for about ½ minute per yolk or until not quite firm in the center. (You'll have to check progress after one yolk's worth of time.) Stir, let stand until firm, then chop or mash.

likings. Cross my heart, birds have eaten, before witnesses, kippered herring, pickles, sauerkraut, mushrooms, fried fish, canned corn, buttermilk, jam, stolen dog and cat food, and shelled green peas, among other things. And that's not counting what they're learning to eat, even as we speak, in the parking lots of fast-food joints . . .

Not so odd and in fact nutritionally sound is their eating of straight salt (their systems need it), mud (probably for its grit), eggshells (including those of other birds' eggs), bits of mortar from brickwork, charcoal and ashes — all good sources of grit and minerals.

Suet, Fresh & Rendered

———◆———

Suet is the solid fat from a beef carcass, although the name is sometimes misapplied to fat from other meat critters. (Sheep fat is called tallow; pig fat is plain pork fat or lard.) Suet is our best ally in making friends among tree-clinging, insect-eating birds such as woodpeckers, flickers, creepers and nuthatches, as well as those that consume a more mixed diet (titmice and chickadees, for instance). Suet is high on the insectivores' preferred menu at any time of year and is often taken by normally "vegetarian" birds when they're rearing young.

The top quality "classic suet" is from the kidney area — ivory-white and firm, with few if any blotches, membranes, blood spots or glands; it comes from the cavity of the carcass. (Kidney suet is a classic ingredient of "people" food in dishes such as steamed Christmas puddings.) Usually this suet can be put into feeders just as it comes from the butcher, with no need for cleanup trimming.

Available more often than the top quality is beef fat from other parts of the carcass. Fat trimmed from wholesale cuts by the butcher or cut at home from overfatty steaks and roasts is fine for rendering. It's softer in texture and usually discolored externally and interrupted by membranes and various glands. If it's to be fed in the chunk, it will keep better (and be less attractive to varmints) after it's trimmed of such bad bits.

FEEDING FRESH SUET. Hang chunks in your Bird Feed Bag or put into any other suet holder, store-bought or home-devised (see "Custom-made Feeders for Bird Delicacies," beginning on page 117). Wedging suet between forking branches of a tree is fine unless raccoons or possums come roaming — if they're in the neighborhood, the suet will be gone before morning if you forget to bring it in at night.

How to Render Suet

To "render" suet is to melt the pure fat free of the membranes that weave around, over and through it. (That's what our pioneer forebears did to get the makings of soft soap.) Rendered suet is first choice for most bird recipes calling for fat. Shortening, drippings and lard are good substitutes.

PREPARATION: Suet-melting goes fastest if the trimmed raw suet is chopped in a meat grinder, in a food processor pulsed on and off rapidly, or with a knife on a board.

EQUIPMENT: A microwave oven renders suet with pleasing speed, but you have to keep an eye on the proceedings. A slow-cooker needs no watching to speak of, but it will take several hours to do the job. The classic method is to use a pot over low rangetop heat or in the oven.

GENERAL METHOD: Use a heavy, covered pot over medium heat; put half an inch of water with the suet to start things off. When a good layer of fat has emerged, uncover and continue cooking over low heat, stirring occasionally. There will be much bubbling while moisture is cooking away. When bubbling stops, most of the fat has cooked out, and browning will begin if you continue to cook. Strain through a sieve set over a bowl, pressing the cracklings to mash out all possible fat. Save the bits for Crackling Cakes (page 89).

OVEN METHOD: Set the pot in a 350°F. oven. Stir occasionally and set the lid ajar after fat has begun to run. Count on 2 to 3 hours' cooking, depending on the quantity of suet.

YIELD: Rendered suet weighs about 20% less than the raw material. A quart (about 2 pounds) of rendered suet will make a dozen muffin-size pure suet cakes (2¾ inches).

TO STORE: Fresh suet may be refrigerated up to 2 weeks, rendered suet almost indefinitely; both can be frozen for several months.

Coconut Cakes

SEASON: Cool or cold weather; okay in warmer weather if placed in shade.

FEEDER: Bag, cake basket or suet holder, can/pans, coconut shell, feeder log.

METHOD AND TIME: No cooking (except to warm fat); 5 minutes if canned coconut is used (longer, depending on dexterity, for fresh coconut).

YIELD: About 1 pound.

Toss grated or chopped coconut, as is, onto the feeding table for an occasional treat. Sweetened coconut is fine, if that's what you have — birds *do* possess the avian equivalent of a "sweet tooth."

If you're using a fresh coconut, choose one that sounds sloshy when shaken. (No liquid means the coconut is going downhill.)

2 cups white vegetable shortening, lard or rendered suet (page 80), warmed slightly to soften
4 cups packaged coconut (2 packages, 7 ounces each) or 1 fresh coconut, grated

Warm fat slightly in a pan or skillet. Finely chop the coconut in a food processor or on a board with a sharp knife. Mash coconut and fat together thoroughly. (This can be speeded up by stirring the combination briefly over low heat.)

Make muffin-pan cakes or a loaf, or pack the mixture into the holes of a feeding log or into a coconut shell (see "Coconut-Shell Cups") or small cans or pie pans. Chill until firm.

COCONUT-SHELL CUPS

Saw a coconut in half crosswise, pry out the sweet meat for kitchen use (or use it for Coconut Cakes) and use the shell halves as feeders.

For each cup: drill a small hole ½ inch from the rim, put a fat knot in the end of a strong hanging cord, and pass the cord through the hole from the inside. Pack the shell with any rich bird food mixture that suits you and hang it from a tree limb, stretched wire or bracket.

Durable coconut shells last for several seasons.

To serve: Hang chunks in your Bird Feed Bag, or put into a suet holder. Nail small cans or pie pans of coconut cake to a post or tree. Hang coconut shell.

To store: Refrigerate, wrapped, up to a week, or freeze up to 2 months.

HOW TO CRACK A COCONUT. Pierce two of the "eyes" with an ice pick and drain out the liquid. If you plan to use the shell halves as bird-feeding bowls, hacksaw the coconut in half, then pry out the meat with a blunt knife; otherwise, crack the nut into chunks with a hammer, then dig out the meat. It's not necessary to pare the brown skin from the meat before grating.

Myth 8

Untimely Feeding Can Keep Birds from Migrating When They Should

Can seasonal migrants, such as hummingbirds, be enticed by the availability of summer feeders (nectar feeders, in their case) to hang around dangerously late when they should be on their way to winter quarters? *Facts:* Experts say this isn't so; birds know very well when to leave, and an occasional lingerer doesn't prove the contrary—it's probably ailing. *Grain of Truth:* Each year there is word of birds nesting and often wintering over in areas where they were formerly rare or not known, no doubt as part of a northward drift of species during a warming climatic trend. (We ourselves have a resident pair of red-bellied woodpeckers and a number of tufted titmice and Carolina wrens, none of which used to be seen in these parts in winter.) Such "new" species appreciate feeders but don't depend on handouts any more than old residents do. If a bird of a kind that migrates infallibly and punctually stays behind, it's almost certainly sick or hurt; it hasn't been misled by a good meal.

Thou'lt break my heart, thou warbling bird, That wantons through the flowering thorn; Thou minds me o' departed joys, Departed never to return.

—Robert Burns, "The Banks o' Doon"

Rib-Sticking Corn Bread

SEASON: Year round.

FEEDER: Bag, cake basket or suet holder, bird table, ground.

METHOD & TIME: Stovetop (to melt the fat), oven; 45 to 60 minutes.

YIELD: 1 large or 2 smaller panfuls.

This "bird" version of corn bread is taken eagerly in chunks or as crumbs, and is an excellent food (far better than store-bought bread) in any season. In very cold weather, you can ratchet up its nutritiousness by adding nuts to the batter.

◆

½–⅔ cup bacon or other drippings, lard or vegetable shortening, or ½ cup vegetable oil (recycled is fine)
3 cups yellow cornmeal
1 cup all-purpose flour (half whole-wheat flour may be used)
3 teaspoons baking powder
3½ cups milk (reconstituted dried milk is okay) or water
Optional: *1 cup chopped nutmeats (any kind), peanuts (any kind) or peanut hearts*

◆

Preheat the oven to 350°F. Melt the fat or oil in a 10- or 11-inch ovenproof skillet, or melt it in any small pan and use some to grease a 9 × 13-inch oblong baking pan or two 8-inch square pans.

Whisk together the cornmeal, flour and baking powder. In a separate bowl, combine the fat or oil with the liquid; stir

SUMER IS ICUMEN IN — FOOD FOR WARM WEATHER

We need to make only a few changes in our bird-catering once spring has declared itself. As our birds of summer arrive from the South to stay, and other species pass through on their way to nesting territory farther north, our main job is keeping up with their appetites after their long trip. So for a while it's the same foods as before but in greater quantity.

Once migration is over and things have settled down, around mid-May, the birds will seem to have thinned out with the scattering of mated pairs to local nesting sites. (There will actually be more birds around than in winter, but except when they raise their voices at dawn, this can be hard to believe.) Busy breeders won't be seen much for a while except when they make hit-and-run raids on feeders to supple-

into dry ingredients just to moisten. Add nuts. Scrape into prepared pan(s).

Bake 40 to 50 minutes, or until corn bread is moderately browned and starts to shrink from pan sides. Let cool in pan(s).

To serve: Hang slabs in your Bird Feeder Bag, put into a suet holder, or crumble for the feeding table or ground-feeding area.

To store: Refrigerate, wrapped, up to a week, or freeze up to 2 months.

Baked Hoecake

SEASON: Year round.

FEEDER: Bag, cake basket or suet holder, bird table, ground.

METHOD & TIME: Oven; 35 to 40 minutes.

YIELD: About 2 pounds.

T he ancestor of our more delicate corn breads is the hoecake, originally baked on a hoe blade. This avian version, concocted of the same ingredients, keeps the usual measure of salt — it does no harm to birds and they sometimes seek it out; in fact, some feeding stations regularly offer dishes of coarse salt as an "extra."

◆

Bacon or other drippings, or any kind of fat, for greasing pan
4 cups yellow cornmeal
2 teaspoons salt
3 cups boiling water, more if needed
Optional: *Bacon or other drippings to enrich the finished cake*

◆

ment their wild foods. When the eggs have hatched into hungry young, feeder business will pick up again, not to decline until migrants take off in early fall.

As the weather warms up, all but a couple of suet feeders will go out of business and we'll take care that the remaining suet never becomes rancid. (If necessary, it is moved into day-long shade.) Corn and peanut hearts will be cut out in the warm months.

Two sunflower feeders (one for seed, one for chopped sunflower meats) will be kept filled, as will the tube feeder for niger (thistle) seed, which comes into its own as a magnet for goldfinches in early summer. Diners at the bird table will find mixed seed, crumbs, nutmeats and fruit. When hatching has begun (listen for the squawks of babies begging to be fed), the table should offer soft foods that parents can take back to the hatchlings (page 87).

The best of the many rewards of summer feeding will come when the fledglings begin to fly. Then (at our place) clamoring young titmice, finches, chickadees, cardinals and

Preheat the oven to 425°F. Grease a jelly-roll pan (about 10 × 15 inches), using drippings or other fat.

Stir meal and salt together. Make a hollow in the center and slowly pour in most of the boiling water, stirring with a fork; if all the cornmeal hasn't been moistened, add a little more water. The dough should be damp, neither crumbly nor dripping wet. Rinsing your hands in water as necessary, pat dough into the pan. Prick dough all over with a fork.

Bake hoecake until it shrinks from the pan sides and is lightly browned, about 30 minutes. Optionally, to enrich the hoecake, heat a few tablespoons of bacon or other drippings and drizzle over the cake. Let cool.

To serve: Crumble and scatter on the feeding table or ground-feeding area, or hang chunks in your Bird Feed Bag.

To store: Bag or wrap in plastic; keep at room temperature for 2 or 3 days, refrigerate up to a week, or freeze up to 2 months.

perhaps even wood-peckers (we've had baby red-bellies) will come to one feeder or another with their parents, begging to be fed with raucous voices and fluttering little stubs of wings. They've actually been fetched to school, a safe spot where they can learn to feed themselves. Here the parents show the young, by alternate feeding and neglect, *"This is where the food is — now go to it, Junior."*

Cranberry Hasty Pudding

SEASON: Cool or cold weather.

FEEDER: Bag, cake basket or suet holder, cans/pans, feeder log, milk carton.

METHOD & TIME: Stovetop; about 20 minutes.

YIELD: About 4 pounds.

The puppy biscuits in this recipe aren't to be sniffed at — they add valuable nutrients. When buying, look on the box

These are the days when birds come back,
A very few, a bird or two,
To take a backward look.
—*Emily Dickinson, "Indian Summer"*

for percentages of protein and fat. Biscuits of the best quality contain around 30% protein, 20% fat.

◆

*2–2½ cups (about a pound) chopped
   or ground fresh suet
½ cup salad oil (recycled is fine)
1 cup sugar (any kind)
2 cups yellow cornmeal
3 cups water, or more if needed
2 cups cranberries**
*1 cup peanut hearts, chopped peanuts
   (and kind) or nutmeats (any kind)
1½ cups crumbled high-protein puppy
   biscuits*

◆

Combine suet, oil and sugar in a big pot; stir. In a bowl, combine the cornmeal and water; add to pot. Add cranberries and nuts.

Cook over medium heat, stirring constantly, until quite thick (about 5 minutes' simmering after it boils). If too thick to stir (unlikely), add a little more water. Remove from heat; stir in the puppy biscuits.

Mold into cupcakes, loaves or a flat pan, or pack into cans or small pie pans. Chill.

To serve: Hang cupcakes or chunks in your Bird Feed Bag, or put into a suet holder. Tack filled cans or pie pans to a post or tree.

To Store: Refrigerate, well wrapped, up to a week, or freeze up to 2 months.

* Dried currants, raisins, blueberries, or other dried fruit can replace cranberries in seasons of scarcity. Soak dried fruit in hot tap water for a few minutes before using.

BABY FOOD

Once nesting season is well under way, it's helpful to put out soft foods for parents to take to hatchlings in the nest. (Suet in your regular feeders will be well patronized at this time, even by birds that don't ordinarily eat it — it's good growing-food for the young.) Some thoughts: shallow dishes of bread crumbs in milk (some birds will drink the liquid), scrambled or mashed hard-cooked eggs, Bacon & Eggs, good-quality canned dog or cat food, broken-up cooked mush, finely chopped cooked meat, cottage cheese, and soft-cooked dried peas or lentils.

Eggshell & Suet Cakes

SEASON: Year round, but most valuable in nesting season.

FEEDER: Bag, cake basket or suet holder.

METHOD & TIME: Stovetop (warming only); 3 minutes.

YIELD: About 2½ pounds.

Wild birds need minerals (especially calcium) year round, but their need is greatest at nesting season. Recycled eggshells furnish calcium for free, and it's easy to form the habit of accumulating them for your recipes for the birds. The feeling is virtuous.

A mineral alternative to eggshells is fine poultry grit made from oyster shells, obtainable at (where else?) feed stores. Grit can replace eggshells in our recipes, in addition to being offered in a shallow dish or in a separate spot in the feeding station—birds take grit to serve as grinding stones in the crop.

◆

1 cup crushed eggshells (see below)
2 cups (1 pound) rendered suet (page 80), warmed to soften

◆

Stir together shells and suet. Mold into small cakes (muffins) or a loaf.

To serve: Hang in your Bird Feed Bag, or put into a suet holder.

To store: Refrigerate for a month or more, or freeze up to several months.

CRUSHED EGGSHELLS. Rinse out the shells of freshly broken eggs; scrape any rem-

TRUE GRIT(S)

Bird gizzards are different from human stomachs because they require the presence of a grinding agent — sand or fine gravel, for instance — in order to process food to a digestible consistency. So, when birds sometimes seem to be eating busily from the ground, they're actually picking up the day's ration of grit.

The well-supplied dining area thus includes a dish or heap of gritty stuff: coarse sand, oyster-shell grit (sold for feeding poultry), small gravel, crushed eggshell (also valuable for its calcium), fireplace ashes with cinders among them, well-crushed seashells, even broken-up charcoal. Maintaining the grit supply is especially important when snow covers such normal sources as the edges of roads.

nants from the shells of soft-boiled eggs and rinse them; the peelings of hard-cooked eggs are okay as is.

Dry the shells in a warm and/or dry spot for a few hours or a few days, then finely crush them any way that's handy. A food processor works in nanoseconds, but a rolling pin serves. Store indefinitely in a covered jar or can.

Crackling Cakes

SEASON: Cool or cold weather, but acceptable year round.

FEEDER: Bag, cake basket or suet holder, feeder log.

METHOD & TIME: Stovetop (if warming required); 5 minutes.

YIELD: 4 cakes.

This is a waste-not use for the scraps (cracklings) left in the pot after suet has been rendered (page 80). Use the cracklings warm from the pot, or refrigerate and rewarm when making the cakes.

Crackling Cakes are a great delicacy to all our suet-eaters. (Another use for cracklings is to strew them where they'll be found by crows and other ground-feeders that are fond of meaty scraps.)

◆

Cracklings from 2 pounds suet, rendered
½ cup warm rendered suet or other fat

◆

Spoon warm cracklings into muffin cups fitted with paper liners. To cement to-

Freckled nesteggs
thou shalt see
Hatching in the
hawthorn-tree
When the hen-bird's
wing doth rest
Quiet on her mossy
nest . . .
—John Keats, "Fancy"

gether the makings of 4 such "muffins," divide about ½ cup of warm liquid fat (some of the rendered suet, or any kind of drippings) among the cups of cracklings. Chill until solid.

To serve: Hang in your Bird Feed Bag, or put into a suet holder. One or more softened cakes can also be used to fill the holes of a feeder log.

To store: Refrigerate, wrapped, up to a month, or freeze for several months.

Double-Peanut Cakes

SEASON: Year round.

FEEDER: Bag, cake basket or suet holder, cans/pans, milk carton, feeder log, grapevine wreath or globe, suet bell.

METHOD & TIME: Stovetop (to warm fat), otherwise no cooking; 5 minutes.

YIELD: About 2½ pounds.

P eanuts in any form—even in the shell, in the case of blue jays—are much relished by most birds (and so are true nuts, with the black walnut perhaps the No. 1 choice). And no wonder—peanuts and nuts are rich in protein and the fat needed by birds' fast metabolisms. This recipe has a double dip of peanuts, but any nuts you have on hand can be combined with peanut butter in the same way.

❦

3 cups rendered suet (page 80)
2 cups peanuts (any kind) or peanut hearts
1 cup peanut butter (any kind)

❦

❝Nearly all the warblers sing in passing . . . in the orchards, in the groves, in the woods . . . their brief, lisping, shuffling, insect-like notes requiring to be searched for by the ear.❞
—John Burroughs' America

Warm suet in skillet or saucepan. Meanwhile, chop nuts coarsely; mix thoroughly with suet and peanut butter. Mold into cupcakes or loaves, or fill a milk-carton feeder (page 120), small cans or small pie pans. Chill.

Optional extras: Up to 1 cup of millet, sunflower hearts or other seed may be included.

To serve: Hang cakes or chunks in your Bird Feed Bag or put into a suet holder; tack cans or pie pans to a post or tree. The mixture can also be stored in a coffee can or other container for refilling log feeders or used to make a suet bell.

To store: Refrigerate, wrapped, up to 4 weeks, or freeze for several months.

Sugared Doughnuts

SEASON: Cool or cold weather, but acceptable all year.

FEEDER: Doughnut tree or spike.

METHOD & TIME: Stovetop; 1 hour or less.

YIELD: 2 dozen 2¾-inch doughnuts.

B irds (especially, in our yard, the tufted titmice) like the sweet taste of doughnuts (and they benefit from the fat).

The art of doughnut-making at home isn't thriving in these busy-busy days, but "donut" stores *are*, and every supermarket sells sinkers (check the penny-saving table of day-old goods). If you like to cook, this no-frills recipe will make a big trayful for a fragment of their price at the local

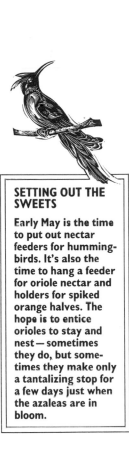

SETTING OUT THE SWEETS

Early May is the time to put out nectar feeders for hummingbirds. It's also the time to hang a feeder for oriole nectar and holders for spiked orange halves. The hope is to entice orioles to stay and nest—sometimes they do, but sometimes they make only a tantalizing stop for a few days just when the azaleas are in bloom.

doughnuttery. A bonus: You can eat some yourself — the ingredients are standard items, and flavorings have been included.

◆

1 egg
⅔ cup sugar
¼ cup soft vegetable shortening
⅔ cup milk
1 teaspoon vanilla
3 cups all-purpose flour
3 teaspoons baking powder
½ teaspoon salt
⅓ teaspoon ground or grated nutmeg
*   or mace*
For frying: *Vegetable oil or shortening*
For coating: *Confectioners' sugar*

◆

Beat egg and sugar together until well blended. (An electric mixer can do the whole recipe.) Beat in shortening, then milk and vanilla.

Sift together the dry ingredients and add to the liquid mixture, beating slowly just until well blended. Optionally, refrigerate the dough for 1 hour.

On a lightly floured surface, pat the dough out to a thickness of ⅓ to ½ inch. Cut out with a medium-size doughnut cutter (or a plain round cutter, plus a tiny round cutter or bottle cap for removing the centers). Gather the scraps and cut more doughnuts until all the dough has been cut.

Heat a 3-inch depth of frying fat in a deep-frying kettle (or flat-bottomed wok) to 375°F. Slip in a few doughnuts (2 to 6, depending on the fryer size) and fry 2 to 3 minutes or until moderately brown; turn and cook until done. Remove each doughnut, when ready, to paper towels. Recheck the temperature of fat before each additional batch.

❝*For, lo, the winter is past, the rain is over and gone; The flowers appear on the earth; the time of the singing of birds is come, and the voice of the turtle is heard in our land . . .***❞**
—*Song of Solomon 2:11, 12*

If some of the doughnuts are for yourself, shake confectioners' sugar over them while warm. I like to sugar-coat doughnuts for the birds, too — the white coating may help them discover the unfamiliar pastry more quickly, as they are attracted to white foods.

To serve: Hang one or two doughnuts on tree twigs, or on the hook of a stretched-out wire coat hanger attached upside down to the wire supporting other feeders. Or, put them onto a doughnut spike feeder, or onto a nail tapped into a post, and wait for them to be discovered.

To store: Wrap and store in a canister for a day or two at room temperature, refrigerate for several days, or freeze for a month or more.

Quick Fresh Suet & Seed Cakes

SEASON: Cool or cold weather.

FEEDER: Bag, cake basket or suet holder, pans/cans, feeder log, milk carton, coconut shell, grapevine wreath or globe, suet bell.

METHOD & TIME: Stovetop; 15 minutes.

YIELD: About 2¾ pounds.

PLAIN SUET CAKES

Store-bought suet cakes, plain or enhanced, are widely available. They're convenient products, but custom-making such cakes is quick and simple, as the recipes demonstrate.

A cost comparison: Suet cakes cost from 2 to 3 dollars per pound. For whatever your butcher charges for suet (we usually get 2 or 3 pounds for a dollar) plus the value of your kitchen services, you'll have both a bargain and fresher bird food, *sans* preservatives, which are found in some store-bought suet cakes.

This rich winter warmer for the flocks can be made quickly even without a food processor. The only real work involved is chopping the suet; after that, it's mostly a stir or two over the heat.

You'll notice that this formula has a

little of almost everything on the birds' all-time-hit food list. It's hard to exaggerate the winter need for solid nourishment from fat (equivalent to insects in the "wild" diet), grain and seeds. The sugar is a lagniappe, one much liked by dozens of species; sweet stuff isn't for the nectar-feeders alone.

◆

3½ cups (1½ pounds) fresh suet or beef-fat trimmings, cubed
1½ cups peanut hearts or peanuts (any kind)
1 cup rolled oats (any kind)
1½ cups sunflower meats
1 cup fine-cracked corn or coarse-ground yellow cornmeal
¾ cup sugar (any kind)

◆

In days when daisies deck the ground,
And blackbirds whistle clear
With honest joy our hearts will bound,
To see the coming year.
—Robert Burns, "Epistle to Davie, a Brother Poet"

Combine fat, nuts and oats in a food processor; pulse on and off rapidly to chop to a rough, chunky mass, not a paste. (This can also be done with a long, sharp knife on a board.)

Heat in a saucepan, stirring, just until the fat begins to run freely. Remove from heat, and stir in remaining ingredients.

Mold into muffin shapes or loaves, or pack into cans or small pie pans.

To serve: Hang peeled "muffins" or a chunk of loaf in your Bird Feed Bag or put into a suet holder. Fasten cans or pie pans to posts or trees. Or pack some of the mixture (warm to soften, if necessary) into a log feeder, milk-carton feeder, coconut half, or any other feeder that accommodates mixtures rather than blocks. The mixture can also be used to make a suet bell.

To store: Refrigerate up to 2 weeks, or freeze up to 2 months.

Fresh & Dried Fruits

Famous fruit-eaters include orioles, tanagers, catbirds and mockingbirds, but others — robins, cardinals, thrushes, rose-breasted grosbeaks and brown thrashers — also pounce on fresh fruit and, often, soaked dried fruit, too. Because of its juiciness, fruit is especially welcome in summer on the feeding table, but it will be gladly taken in other seasons.

SERVING FRESH FRUIT: Put halved apples, crabapples, oranges or pears on the bird table, spike them on tree twigs, or place on an orange spike. Bananas, skin stripped from the top, go on the table, as do berries or slightly mashed grapes in shallow dishes. Grapefruit isn't highly popular in itself (too tart?), but the emptied halves are ready-made bowls for fruit mixtures (below). Save and serve fresh melon seeds in a flat dish; scoop watermelon pulp into a saucer, or leave it attached to the rind for do-it-yourself pecking.

DRIED FRUIT: Soak dried currants, raisins, blueberries (or other berries), sliced prunes, and any other cut-up dried fruit (apples, pears, cherries, apricots, peaches) in a shallow dish of water for a couple of hours before placing on the bird table, juice and all.

FOR FRUIT SALAD: Cut up oranges, grapes, apples, berries, bananas, melon (any kind) in any feasible combination. Put, with the juice, into an emptied grapefruit or melon half.

You can also include cut-up prunes, figs or dates, or dried currants or raisins. Leave the fruit out as long as it's edible in bird terms (softening or browning doesn't bother them), but remove leftovers before mold or rot sets in.

Fruited Oat Bread

SEASON: Year round.

FEEDER: Bag, cake basket or suet holder, bird table.

METHOD & TIME: Oven (and stovetop); about 30 minutes.

YIELD: About 1½ pounds.

The good grains, some milk, some fruit, and a little fat add up to a nourishing food to crumble onto the bird table or put out in chunks for pecking.

---

2 cups whole-wheat or all-purpose flour
2 cups rolled oats (any kind)
4 teaspoons baking powder
1 cup raisins, currants or chopped pitted prunes
2 eggs
1¼ cups milk (reconstituted dried milk is fine)
6 tablespoons salad oil, drippings (warmed until soft) or recycled oil

---

Preheat the oven to 375° F. Grease two 8- or 9-inch layer-cake or square pans.

Stir together flour, oats, baking powder and dried fruit. In a separate bowl, beat the eggs with the milk, then beat in the oil or drippings; stir into the dry ingredients. Spread batter in prepared pans and bake about 20 minutes or until firm and barely browned. Let cool in the pan or on a rack.

To serve: Hang chunks in your Bird Feed Bag, or crumble for the bird table.

To store: Refrigerate, wrapped, up to a week, or freeze up to 2 months.

When the blue
summer night
Is short and safe
and light,
Why should the
starlings any
more remember
The fearful,
trembling times of
dark December?
—*Mary Webb, "The Starling"*

Kush-Kush Crumble

SEASON: Year round, but especially cool or cold weather.

FEEDER: Bird table or ground.

METHOD & TIME: Stovetop; 10 to 15 minutes.

YIELD: About 5 cups.

The southern dish called kush-kush inspired this quick, crumbly treat for the bird table. It's a neat way to recycle bacon (or other) drippings, and it doesn't require premium-quality cornmeal — something off the supermarket shelf will be fine.

◆

*³/₄ cup bacon or other drippings, or
    rendered suet (page 80)
2 cups yellow cornmeal
2 teaspoons baking powder (optional
    but recommended)
2 cups water*

◆

Melt the fat in a skillet over medium heat. Meanwhile, stir together the remaining ingredients.

When fat is hot but not smoking, pour in the batter. When it has set around the sides, stir and turn the mixture with a spatula for 2 or 3 minutes, until it resembles scrambled eggs.

Cover pan, lower heat and cook 2 to 4 minutes longer, until the grains have swollen and the mixture is stiff. Spread on a platter to cool.

Optional additions: Add a handful of crushed eggshells (page 88) or ½ cup chopped peanuts to the batter, or stir in

❝Delighted surprise is felt by everyone, I imagine, when he learns . . . that our little brown creeper is a singer.**❞**
—Bradford Torrey,
Birds in the Bush

½ cup peanut butter at the end of cooking.

To serve: Crumble and scatter on the bird table or over the ground-feeding area.

To store: Bag and refrigerate up to a week or freeze up to 2 months.

Meatballs from Bits & Pieces

SEASON: Cool or cold weather.

FEEDER: Bag, cake basket or suet holder, feeder log, suet bell.

METHOD & TIME: Stovetop; 30 to 40 minutes.

YIELD: Depends on desired amount.

You've trimmed a roast, or cuts for the freezer, or suet to be rendered, and you're left with scraps of good fresh meat; or you have a remnant of hamburger, not enough to freeze and too good to waste. Will your bird population be interested? Yes, say our winter yard birds. The nuthatches, titmice, woodpeckers, chickadees and brown creepers like cooked meat very much, especially when it's mixed with suet. For future meatballs, we accumulate trimmings in the freezer until we have enough for a batch.

❖

Chopped or ground meat trimmings or hamburger
About half as much rendered suet (page 80) or drippings as meat
Mixed birdseed, or sunflower meats or millet

❖

Place trimmings or hamburger in saucepan with an inch of water; simmer, cov-

A BIRD'S-EYE LOOK AT COLORS

The color of food *does* count, up to a point, in attracting birds to your dining areas, particularly the food put on the bird table and in nectar feeders.

We've found that a little diced white bread is the best advertisement and lure for something new we've put on the table — say, freshly bought safflower seed that we want to call to the attention of cardinals, or something else, such as crumbled Fruited Oat Bread, that's really nutritious but, because of its modest tan color, is less likely than white bread to be pounced on.

Why not just settle for feeding white bread instead of making it the fan in a fan dance? Well, even a good white loaf is relatively low in bird nutrients and should be used only sparingly as a food item. But once a come-hither offering of white bread is gone, the good stuff it's advertising will be tried by birds that will almost certainly come back for more.

To a bird's eye,

ered, over low heat about 30 minutes or until very soft. Uncover toward the end to let any liquid evaporate.

Microwave: Microwave the meat with a little water, covered, at full power for 10 minutes for about a pound (adjust the time for more or less weight), stirring once or twice. Check, and cook longer if necessary; the meat should be soft. Drain any surplus liquid.

Add fat and blend. If mixture is too oily, add a handful of the seed (or cornmeal or flour).

To shape: Pack into muffin pans fitted with paper liners or into a loaf pan, or mold a suet bell (page 127).

To serve: Roll peeled "muffins" or chunks of loaf in seed to form balls. Hang in your Bird Feed Bag, or put into a suet holder. Coat the suet bell with seed (optional) and hang it out. This mixture is also good for filling the cavities of a feeder log.

To store: Refrigerate, wrapped, up to 5 days, or freeze up to 2 months.

Come-Hither Nectar for Hummingbirds & Orioles

SEASON: Hummingbird and oriole time (spring to early fall, but including winter in mild regions).

FEEDER: Nectar holder.

METHOD & TIME: Stovetop; 3 minutes, plus cooling time.

YIELD: About 1 pint.

red foods are the next most attractive after white. This is most striking with hummingbirds, which prefer red flowers as natural nectar sources and will therefore buzz up for a drink of plain sugar water (below) if the feeder is decked out with red trimming.

Oriole nectar offered in special feeders is often flavored with orange extract and tinted, too, to increase its allure. Are these touches necessary? Experts aren't certain. Orioles (and tanagers, too, I hear — we haven't had any yet) certainly love real orange halves (so do finches, and squirrels) and come to them avidly (see page 129). The color yellow, as in corn and corn bread, is also an appetizing one to many species.

After white, red and orange foods, the color of brownish things — nutmeats and peanuts, for instance — seems to be next most attractive. Then come black items. Black is rare at the feeder except for niger and black-oil sunflower seeds, one of the favorite foods of stout-billed seed-eaters like cardinals and daintier birds such as chickadees and finches.

Nectar for hummingbirds used to be routinely tinted with red food coloring, but that's done less now because of doubts about the wholesomeness of certain red colorings. You can suit yourself, but hummingbirds will locate clear syrup readily if the feeder is ornamented with the color red, especially around the openings where they sip. Red ribbons, artificial flowers, or nail enamel will do the trick.

Sugar water also attracts orioles (plus, sometimes, other birds that will surprise you) when offered in nectar feeders. For a few pennies you can keep a special feeder filled with this mixture in place of serving pricey packaged oriole foods, which contain "natural orange flavor" and added color as well as occasional preservatives and "vitamins and minerals" that may or may not be useful to birds. If you want to flavor and tint your oriole nectar, add a mere dribble of bottled orange flavoring and a drop or two of yellow coloring and a drop or two of red.

The question of honey: a warning. It's safest not to use it. Some experts say diluted honey may be fed to birds *if great attention is paid to feeder sanitation,* but it doesn't seem worth the risk of causing the well-documented sickness caused by fermentation or the growth of fungus in the honey.

◆

2 cups water
*½ cup granulated sugar**

◆

Bring the water to a boil; stir in the sugar and let the mixture barely return to boiling. Cool, uncovered.

To serve: Be sure hummingbird or oriole feeders are immaculately clean before filling or refilling them.

*The dullest brain, if gently stirr'd,
Perhaps may waken to a hummingbird.*
—Pope

To store: Pour the nectar into a spotless jar, cover and refrigerate. It will be good for several days, or as long as it is clear and shows no specks of incipient fermentation. If you are even slightly in doubt, throw it out.

* Don't let a generous spirit tempt you to increase the sugar in the nectar: more sugar is *not* better in nectar and may in fact be harmful. The proportions in this recipe (4:1) make syrup similar in sweetness to flower nectar, the natural tipple of sweet-loving birds. (In case you were wondering, such birds don't live on nectar alone—they also snack variously on insects, flower buds, tree sap, spiders and fruit.)

NECTAR FEEDERS. These can be purchased or improvised—a small vial or other open container, filled to the brim and hung from a stake among "hummingbird" flowers, will do the trick nicely, especially if decorated with a bit of red. (Paint the edge with nail polish, or tie on a big ribbon bow.)

To prevent untimely fermentation of nectar and/or the formation of molds that can harm the birds, it's vital to wash out and refill the feeders often—at least every 2 or 3 days—especially in warm weather. It's best to change nectar daily if possible; if you rinse out the feeder each time, so much the better.

Once a week or so, and immediately if the old nectar shows the faintest signs of fermentation or mold (look for cloudiness or dark specks), scrub the emptied feeder well with a weak solution of vinegar and water and rinse repeatedly. Pay special attention to any angles on the inside where mold might get a foothold—a small bottle brush helps.

To hear an oriole
sing
May be a common
thing
Or only a divine.
—Emily Dickinson, "The Oriole's Secret"

Plum Pudding

SEASON: Cool or cold weather, but acceptable all year.

FEEDER: Feeder log, milk carton, coconut shell, bag, cake basket or suet holder, cans/pans.

METHOD & TIME: Stovetop; 15 minutes.

YIELD: About 2½ pounds.

*That time of year
thou may'st in
me behold
When yellow leaves,
or none, or few
do hang
Upon those boughs
which shake
against the cold,
Bare ruin'd choirs,
where late the
sweet birds sang.*
—Shakespeare, Sonnet 73

I n this pudding the "plums," true to Christmas tradition, are actually other fruits—your choice. The suety confection is sturdy food for winter birds, who need all the nourishment they can get, and making it is a wonderful warmup for the season of gifts and goodies. For other holiday treats, see "The Birds' Christmas Tree" (page 111).

❖

*2 cups (1 pound) rendered suet
(page 80)
½ cup peanut butter
½ cup brown sugar, packed
1½–2 cups raisins or combined
raisins and chopped dried fruit
(prunes, apples, apricots,
peaches)
1 cup chopped nuts (any kind) or
peanuts
1 cup dry bread crumbs or yellow
cornmeal, or ½ cup of each*

❖

In a large saucepan, warm the suet until it melts to a thick liquid. Stir in the peanut butter and sugar, then mix in the remaining ingredients.

To serve: Pack into a log feeder, milk-carton feeder or coconut shell, make into cakes or a loaf and put chunks into your

Bird Feed Bag or a suet holder. Cans or pans can also be used.

To store: Refrigerate up to 2 weeks or freeze up to 2 months.

String popcorn balls with a big needle and strong thread.

Nutty Popcorn Balls

SEASON: Winter (especially for the birds' Christmas tree).

FEEDER: Garlands or balls, bird table.

METHOD & TIME: Stovetop; about 20 minutes.

YIELD: About 2 quarts.

If family fingers are bored with stringing popcorn kernels for the birds' Christmas tree, make these popcorn balls for no (or faster) stringing. The candy is much the same as "people" food; if humans are likely to share it with the birds, make it with shortening or butter and nutmeats or cocktail peanuts in place of rendered suet and peanut hearts.

2 quarts freshly popped corn
¾ cup coarsely chopped cocktail
    peanuts, nutmeats (any kind) or
    peanut hearts
½ cup brown sugar, packed
½ cup light corn syrup
¼ cup shortening, butter or rendered
    suet (page 80)
¼ teaspoon baking soda

Grease a big, shallow pan; spread with popcorn and nuts.

*The yellow year is
hasting to its
close;
The little birds have
almost sung their
last,
Their small notes
twitter in the
dreary blast—
That shrill-piped
harbinger of early
snows . . .*
— Coleridge, "November"

Combine sugar, syrup and fat in a saucepan; heat, stirring, until boiling. Set heat to medium-low, and cook without stirring until a candy thermometer reads 250°F (or use cold-water test, below). Remove from heat; stir in baking soda, and pour at once over the popcorn and nuts. Toss rapidly with a wide spatula until pieces are mostly coated (a few bare spots are okay).

Let candy cool until it can be handled, then squeeze small palmfuls into nubbly balls. Cool completely.

Cold-water candy test: Dribble two or three drops of boiling candy into a cup of cold water. Pinch the sample with your fingers; the candy has reached the right stage when it's firm, almost crisp.

To serve: Fit balls with Christmas-ornament hangers and hang on an outdoor conifer; or string them a few inches apart on coarse thread, using a large needle. Gather up any scraps (or break up part of the candy) for the feeding table.

To store: Keep in an airtight can for up to 3 weeks.

... and now
with treble soft
The redbreast
whistles from a
garden-croft;
And gathering
swallows twitter
in the skies.
—*John Keats, "To Autumn"*

Putting-on-the-Dog Suet "Muffins"

SEASON: Cool or cold weather (place in shade if days are warm).

FEEDER: Bag, cake basket or suet holder, milk carton, feeder log, suet bell.

METHOD & TIME: Stovetop; 15 minutes.

YIELD: About 1½ pounds.

Paper liners make it a cinch to mold "muffins."

Meaty eats are surprisingly popular with birds, many species of which are more carnivorous than they look — even the diminutive hummingbird consumes both insects and spiders as well as nectar. These cakes are good nourishment, too — high-quality dogfood contains more protein than most of the things added to commercial suet cakes.

If the birds ignore the food at first (they can be conservative sometimes), remove it when it threatens to spoil and try again with a fresh batch. Our winter birds caught on fast to this, and yours may too.

1 pound (2 cups) rendered suet
1 can (14 ounces) high-quality canned
dog food (chopped beef, etc.)

In a skillet, heat the suet just until pourable; stir in the dogfood (hard bubbling will follow). Cook over medium-low heat, stirring occasionally, for 10 minutes to get rid of surplus moisture.

Cool until semiliquid, then stir to distribute the meat bits. Mold as "muffins" or as a loaf. Chill.

To make puppy-biscuit muffins: Substitute 1½ cups of crushed, high-quality puppy biscuits for the canned food and omit the cooking. (When buying the biscuits, look for a brand that contains at least 30% protein, 20% fat.)

To serve: Hang muffins or chunks in your Bird Feed Bag, or put into a suet holder. Softened, the mixture is fine for packing into the holes in a log feeder, for filling a milk-carton feeder, or for making a suet bell.

To store: Refrigerate, wrapped, up to a week; freeze up to 2 months.

66*Never look for birds of this year in the nests of the last.***99**
— *Cervantes,* Don Quixote

Peanutty Raisin & Oat Cakes

SEASON: Year round.

FEEDER: Bag, cake basket or suet holder, pans/cans, feeder log or milk carton, coconut shell, grapevine wreath or globe, suet bell.

METHOD & TIME: Stovetop for warming suet (otherwise no-cook); 10 minutes.

YIELD: About 3 pounds.

R ecyclables fit in here — save any kinds of crumbs for this dish, and make use of drippings you've refrigerated with the yard birds in mind. Add peanut butter and your choice of dried fruit and please the species — among them nuthatches, Carolina wrens, chickadees and titmice — that prefer to picnic at tree-mounted or hanging feeders.

◆

> 2 cups rendered suet (page 80) or
>   drippings
> 2 cups raisins, currants, or chopped
>   dried prunes
> 2 cups rolled oats, any kind
> 1 cup dry crumbs (bread, cracker,
>   cake, cereal)
> 1 cup peanut butter, any kind

◆

Melt the fat or drippings in a skillet or saucepan. Meanwhile, combine raisins and oats in a food processor and pulse machine on and off until they are coarsely chopped. (Or chop with a meat grinder, or in a bowl with a half-moon chopper if you possess such a treasure.) Mix in crumbs, soft suet and peanut butter.

Mold into "cupcakes" or loaves, or

The robin and the bluebird, piping loud,
Filled all the blossoming orchards with their glee
The bluebird balanced on some topmost spray,
Flooding with melody the neighborhood.
—Longfellow, "The Birds of Killingworth," in Tales of a Wayside Inn

pack into cans or individual pie pans. Chill.

To serve: Hang cupcakes or chunks in your Bird Feed Bag, or put into a suet holder. Fasten cans or pie pans to a post or tree. Mixture can also be packed into holes of a hanging-log feeder (page 124), or into a milk-carton feeder (page 120) or coconut-shell cup (page 82), or made into a suet bell (page 127).

To store: Refrigerate, wrapped, up to 2 weeks, or freeze up to 2 months.

THE DUST BATH

An amenity that's easy to provide and much appreciated is a spot where birds can dust-bathe by fluffing loose earth through their feathers. (Anyone who's ever seen barnyard chickens knows how much domestic fowl enjoy such soothing baths, too.) Just set aside a patch of soil fairly close to shelter but not close enough to allow a lurking cat to endanger the bathers. Loosen the spot thoroughly with a rake, keep it unsprinkled and unhosed, and sooner or later your dust bowl will be found and used.

Myth 9

A Feeding Station Puts Birds in Danger from Predators

Are birds at feeders doomed to be sitting ducks for hawks and house cats? *Facts:* Not very much, so far as hawks are concerned. Those raptors that prey on other birds aren't all that efficient in their raids, though they naturally go hunting where they see the best prospects. (In the past three months I've seen six swoops through our yard by hawks, just when I've happened to be looking out. Score: small birds, 6; hawks, 0.) Birds know how to react — they vanish with the speed of light or, in the case of some species, freeze.

Cats can be vexing (though we love them and usually have a few) if they happen to be among those felines that like to lurk in the bushes whetting their appetite for anything that flies. This can keep birds away and can get some of them caught if the cat is any good at doing what comes naturally. (Not all cats are.) Your own cat, if a bird-chaser, can be kept indoors or belled, but neighboring cats can't be fenced out. Avoid placing ground food any closer than about 10 feet from any hiding places, and do what you can to promote the belling of local cats. Keeping a dog can help, too.

Raisin & Peanut Cakebread

SEASON: Year round.

FEEDER: Bag, cake basket or suet holder, bird table.

METHOD & TIME: Oven; about 1 hour.

YIELD: About 2½ pounds.

Reasonably rich in fat and absolutely rich in fruit and peanuts, here's a bird bread or cake you can break into chunks and hang in your Bird Feed Bag. Any incidental crumbs, or crumbs made on purpose from part of the bread, are welcomed at the bird table, where species such as finches (some of them), jays, doves, sparrows, cardinals, and the occasional titmouse are our frequent guests.

½ cup rendered suet (page 80) or vegetable shortening
3 cups whole-wheat flour, or half whole wheat, half white
1 cup rolled oats, any kind, or whole-wheat cereal, or cornmeal
½ cup dried milk powder
2 teaspoons baking powder
1 cup peanut hearts or chopped peanuts, any kind
1 cup chopped raisins or currants
1¾ cups water or milk

Preheat the oven to 350°F. Grease a 9 × 13-inch baking pan and dust it with flour. Melt the suet or shortening just until liquid.

Stir together the flour, oats, milk powder and baking powder in a mixing bowl;

CATCHING SOME RAYS

You may notice that an occasional bird chooses to sunbathe on the ground. That's what is going on when you see a bird lying quite still in the sun, wings spread and feathers loosened — disheveled it may be, but dying it's not.

add the nuts and raisins or currants.

Combine the fat with the water or milk; add to dry ingredients and stir just to combine. (The batter will be heavy.) Spread it in the prepared pan.

Bake the cake about 45 minutes, or until firm and lightly browned. Let cool in the pan.

To serve: Hang chunks in your Bird Feed Bag, or put into a suet holder. Alternatively, crumble coarsely for the feeding table.

To store: Wrap and keep at room temperature up to a week, or freeze up to 2 months.

Stovetop Corn Cake

SEASON: Cool or cold weather.

FEEDER: Bag, suet holder, bird table.

METHOD & TIME: Stovetop (or oven); 20 (or 25) minutes.

YIELD: About 2 pounds.

A little gentle heat on the front burner turns out this rich bird bread, which is made with sugar to add appeal and crushed eggshells to contribute minerals and a share of grit. It is one of the most popular foods we offer—our pair of crimson-capped red-bellied woodpeckers comes daily, and even the shy brown creeper has visited it more than once this past winter, when other, bolder birds have permitted. (We think the bacon fat is what fetches 'em.)

CORN ON THE COB AS A SQUIRREL DISTRACTION

To lure squirrels to a feast of their own at a desirable distance from the bird feeders, pound a big, sharp nail (4 inches or longer) through a square of stout board. Impale the base of a dried ear of corn on the spike and nail the board either horizontally or vertically to any convenient surface within reach of squirrels, which means almost anywhere. Don't be surprised if jays patronize your corn, too.

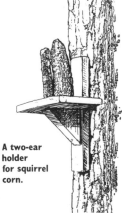

A two-ear holder for squirrel corn.

1 cup bacon or other drippings, or
    rendered suet (page 80)
2½ cups water
2½ cups yellow cornmeal
½–1 cup sugar (any kind)
¼–½ cup crushed eggshells (page 88)
Optional: A handful of rolled oats,
    raisins, currants, chopped
    peanuts, chopped nutmeats or
    crushed puppy biscuits

In a 10- or 11-inch skillet, preferably one with a nonstick lining, heat the bacon fat just until melted.

Meanwhile, stir together the remaining ingredients. Add most of the warm fat, leaving a thin layer in the pan. Mix batter well, then pour it into the pan. Cook until edges begin to firm up; cover and cook over medium-low heat about 15 minutes or until firm. Check occasionally; if fat is floating on top, poke holes in the cake and shake the pan to help it soak in.

Uncover and let cool.

To oven-bake the corn cake: Heat the fat in an ovenproof skillet in a 375°F. oven. Prepare the batter as described; bake until firm, about 25 minutes.

To serve: Hang a chunk in your Bird Feed Bag, put into a suet holder, or crumble and scatter on the bird table.

To store: Refrigerate, wrapped, up to a week, or freeze up to 2 months.

*Thou wast not born
    for death,
    immortal Bird!
No hungry
    generations tread
    thee down;
The voice I hear
    this passing night
    was heard
In ancient days by
    emperor and
    clown:
Perhaps the self-
    same song that
    found a path
Through the sad
    heart of Ruth,
    when, sick for
    home,
She stood in tears
    among the alien
    corn;
The same that
    oftentimes hath
Charmed magic
    casements,
    opening on the
    foam
Of perilous seas, in
    faery lands
    forlorn.*
—John Keats, "Ode to a
Nightingale"

The Birds' Christmas Tree

An outdoor evergreen (or any other tree, or a shrub) hung with bird treats is an old northern European tradition that honors the Nativity. Perhaps most cheering to see when there's snow on the ground, the birds' Christmas tree is welcome to your guests all winter, especially at the tag end. A water supply is equally attractive to birds in freezing weather, so keep that birdbath going. The easy way is by installing a small immersion heater (page 118).

Some Decorations

Garlands of popcorn or fresh cranberries, or large raisins or chunks of other dried fruit, strung on carpet thread. Or string small Nutty Popcorn Balls together.

"Cupcakes" made extra-small; use the directions for Quick Fresh Suet, Seed Cakes, Cranberry Hasty Pudding, Coconut Cakes, Crackling Cakes or Double-Peanut Cakes. For hanging, use needle and string to thread a loop through the cake.

Doughnuts. Make Sugared Doughnuts in any size.

Peanuts or nutmeats, hung in little net sacks.

Suet bells, molded in very small flowerpots.

Stuffed pine cones. Use small cones.

Cubes of bread or cake, impaled on branches or strung.

Chunks of Raisin & Peanut Cakebread, hung in mesh bags. (Or hang Stovetop Corn Cake, Plum Pudding, Rib-Sticking Corn Bread.)

Shortbread & Holiday "Cookies." Bag and hang shortbread chunks; thread hanging loops through cookies.

Fresh suet, hung in small net sacks.

Marshmallows, stuck onto twigs or hung.

Chunks of orange or apple, or other fresh fruit, impaled on twigs or bagged.

Shortbread & Holiday "Cookies"

SEASON: Year round.

FEEDER: Bag, bird table, birds' Christmas tree.

METHOD & TIME: Oven; 40 minutes.

YIELD: About 1 pound.

66And I said, Oh that I had wings like a dove! for then would I fly away, and be at rest.99
—Psalm 55:6

L eftover scraps of pie pastry (any kind) need not go to waste. Just roll or pat them flat and bake a treat for the birds, which will benefit (unlike over-portly humans) from the concentrated fat and carbohydrates. Non-piemakers can toss together this "shortbread," which is sweetened to increase its appeal.

◆

¾ cup vegetable shortening, lard or rendered suet (page 80)
2 cups all-purpose flour
½ cup granulated or (packed) brown sugar
Water or milk, if needed

◆

Preheat the oven to 350°F. Cream the fat. Sift flour and sugar together, then stir into the fat to make a crumbly dough. If it won't hold together when squeezed, sprinkle with 1 tablespoon water or milk, toss with a fork, and squeeze-test again.

On an ungreased cookie sheet, press the dough with your hands to a thickness of about ¼ inch. It needn't be smooth — looks don't count.

Bake until light brown, about 30 minutes. Cool on the pan.

Optional extras: Mix a handful of chopped nuts, peanuts or raisins into the dough for extra nourishment.

To serve: Hang chunks in your Bird Feed Bag; or crumble coarsely for the bird table.

To store: Bag and keep at room temperature up to 3 days, refrigerate up to 2 weeks, or freeze up to several months.

COOKIE ORNAMENTS. To make cookies for the birds' Christmas tree, roll or pat out shortbread dough to a thickness of ¼ inch. Cut cookies into desired shapes. Poke a good-size hole through each cookie to allow for hanging. Bake on a cookie sheet in a 350°F. oven until light brown, about 15 minutes. Cool on rack. Add loops of string for hanging.

"Granola" Bars

SEASON: Cool or cold weather.

FEEDER: Bag, cake basket or suet holder, milk carton, feeder log, grapevine wreath or globe, suet bell.

METHOD & TIME: Stovetop; 15 minutes.

YIELD: About 2½ pounds.

L ike formulas for all the kinds of granola eaten by thee and me, this recipe is nothing if not flexible. Notice the alternatives, all of which your bird guests will eat with alacrity. Use recycled fat, any kind of sunflower seed, canary seed instead of millet, and dried fruit à la carte . . . they'll dine with delight. It's one of the most versatile of our mixtures, too, as it can be served in many ways. You could even chop it up and offer a plateful on the bird table.

That's the wise thrush; he sings each song twice over,
Lest you should think he never could recapture
That first fine careless rapture!
— *Robert Browning, "Home-Thoughts, from Abroad"*

When you want to make bird cakes, mold this mixture in a flat or loaf pan lined with plastic, then chill before cutting it into chunks.

◆

2 cups (1 pound) rendered suet (page 80), bacon or other drippings, or lard
1 cup yellow cornmeal
2 cups sunflower meats or black-oil sunflower seeds, or half and half
1 cup fine-cracked corn
1 cup white millet or canary seed
1 cup grainy cereal (such as Roman Meal or Wheatena) or whole-wheat flour
1 cup raisins, currants or chopped pitted prunes
Optional:
½ cup crushed eggshells (page 88)
½ cup sugar (any kind)

◆

The swallows pass in restless companies.
Against the pink-flowered may, one shining breast Throbs momentary music.
—Mary Webb, ".Swallows"

Warm the fat in a saucepan until pourable. Add all other ingredients and mix well (easiest and smooshiest with the hands).

If mixture is too oily (this depends on the kind of fat), gradually stir in a little additional flour, starting with 2 tablespoons, until surplus fat has been absorbed.

To serve: Make into cakes for your Bird Feed Bag or a fixed suet holder. Or shape into a suet bell, or use mixture while soft (or warm to soften, if it has been refrigerated) to fill a milk-carton feeder or a hanging or fixed log, or to "plaster" a grapevine wreath or grapevine globe.

To store: Refrigerate the granola mixture, wrapped, up to 2 weeks, or freeze up to 2 months.

Tabletop Suet, Corn & Nuts

SEASON: Cool or cold weather.

FEEDER: Bird table or ground.

METHOD & TIME: No cooking; 2 minutes by machine, 10 minutes by hand.

YIELD: About 6 cups.

Coarse yellow cornmeal, if you can find it, gives the best texture to this well-rounded "table" food; ordinary meal will do, however. The suet is for ultra-warming calories, and both cornmeal and nuts add protein and other nutrients (with a bonus of fat from the nuts); so, for those winter birds that prefer to keep their feet on (or near) the ground, it's the equivalent of the rich suet mixtures served in your hanging or tree-mounted feeders.

◆

4 cups yellow cornmeal, preferably coarse-ground
½ pound cubed fresh suet (about 1 cup packed chunks)*
1 cup peanuts, peanut hearts or nuts (any kind)
Optional: *1 cup raisins*

◆

Food-processor method: Put ingredients into the beaker in the order given above. (If the processor is small, divide into two batches for separate processing.) Pulse the machine on and off rapidly until the mixture is crumbly, a matter of a few seconds.

Hand method: Chop the suet on a board (or put it through a meat grinder) to make bits half the size of rice grains.

❝*Each bird loves to hear himself sing.***❞**
—Proverb

Chop (or grind) the nuts and, if desired, the raisins. Blend ingredients by hand or in an electric mixer.

To serve: Scatter on the bird table or over the ground-feeding area.

To store: Bag in plastic or pack into a surplus coffee can. Refrigerate up to 2 weeks, or freeze up to 2 months.

* Use suet that's free of meaty or bloody bits; lacking such, use rendered suet (page 80).

The crow doth sing as sweetly as the lark,
When neither is attended; and I think
The nightingale, if she should sing by day,
When every goose is cackling, would be thought
No better a musician than the wren.

—*Shakespeare,* The Merchant of Venice, *Act V*

Custom-made Feeders for Bird Delicacies

F eeders for foods made from recipes in this book (or feeders for the basic bird-seed and grains discussed on page 50) can be store-bought or home-crafted. Countless ingenious designs are available from hardware stores, garden centers, bird shops and mail-order specialists, and they are mostly very good value. But here, for do-it-yourselfers, are constructive ideas for serving up your home cooking. Any table, or the screen-bottomed feeding table on page 125, is good for seeds and grains as well as cut-up fruits, homemade foods meant to be crumbled, and the like.

Your feeders will be most attractive if you use natural-looking materials when possible—make use of rough-sawed or weathered wood, coconut shells, pine cones, wreaths or balls of grapevine, tree branches or log sections, overlays of bark, and so on. If plastic, metal and smooth wood can't be avoided, their look can sometimes be softened by a camouflage

Sweet is the breath of morn, her rising sweet, With charm of earliest birds . . .
—*Milton,* Paradise Lost, Book *IV*

of bark, rough wood or other unobtrusive material. If not, not. The birds certainly won't mind how a feeder looks if you don't.

Before the feeders comes water. Clean drinking and bathing water, made available winter and summer, will bring more birds than any selection of foods you could possibly offer. (In winter birds *can* derive moisture from snow and even ice if they must, but it's hard on them, as is a rainless period at any time of year.) After sipping, first-timers almost always stay around (or come back) to sample your cuisine and decide how many stars it rates. In any case, repeat business is assured. Birds bathe in winter, too—just watch.

In the absence of a garden pool, a drinking place can be a fairly fancy birdbath designed for the purpose, perhaps with a spray or a waterfall, or it can be something very simple, such as one or two large potted-plant saucers of terra cotta or red-brown plastic; 15 or 18 inches is a good size. Even a metal garbage-can lid, inverted, can be pressed into service. The spa can be placed on the ground (the best level), on a low table or stumplike slice of log, or on the deck— wherever you think the birds can find the water most easily, remembering that they're accustomed to drinking and bathing at puddle level. A spot in partial shade is desirable in hot places (or hot weather). Birds don't like murky water if they can find fresh, so keep an eye on the birdbath and change the water before it even thinks of becoming dirty. The dish will need an occasional strong hosing or scrub-out to remove slime or algae.

Winter warmth. In any place where the temperature goes below freezing, a

GIMME SHELTER

If you live in snow country, you might think about sheltering a winter dining area to keep food accessible in all weather for birds that feed on the ground. A feeding shed is especially helpful to quail and pheasants, which don't like to venture far into the open unless they must.

A feeding shed can be as makeshift as a picnic table moved to an area 10 feet or so from shrubs, brush or other back-up shelter; or you can build a post-supported low roof or slanted lean-to about 3 feet high at the front, which should face south toward the winter sun. The roof can be a half-sheet (4 × 4 feet) of weatherproof plywood or, more attractively, a thick thatch of evergreen branches or leafy cornstalks.

small birdbath immersion heater is a necessity. There are several excellent designs on the market; they use very little electricity to keep the water above freezing, not actually warm, and they're perfectly safe to use.

Your Own Bird Feed Bag

Additional mesh bags for bird food, along the lines of the Bird Feed Bag packaged with this book, can be devised from recycled or purchased materials. Such bags will serve for a couple of seasons if there are no predations by sharp-toothed varmints, and bagging and hanging suitable kinds of bird food is the quickest way to get slabs, balls or chunks, or nutmeats or peanuts within beak's reach of species that love suety things — woodpeckers, titmice, chickadees, and nuthatches especially.

Serviceable material will be found in mesh onion or orange bags recycled from the kitchen; simply drop in the food, tie a knot, and hang. If such bags don't come your way but you're able to sew a (not too) fine seam, shop for some strong, coarse-meshed nylon curtain material and stitch up a bag with a folded-over top to accommodate a drawstring. Strong mason's cord (from the hardware store) makes excellent drawstrings and can be used for hanging, too.

A tepee design is good, too. Make a tepee frame of 3 or 4 poles from 4 to 5 feet long, lashing them together near their tips and setting their bases firmly against the ground. Cover the top half with a thatch of evergreen branches, wired together for stability, or make a conical roof of cornstalks similarly wired together. Be sure there's plenty of room below the roof edge for entrances and exits.

The floor of the shelter will need an occasional raking to get rid of hulls and other debris, both so the birds can find their food and to prevent the risk of disease from decaying leftovers or rubbish.

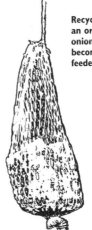

Recycling: an orange or onion bag becomes a feeder.

Milk-Carton Feeder:

Improving on a Kids' Project

Mesh offers a clawhold on this feeder.

Recycling a milk carton to make a feeder is a familiar craft project for children who'd like to attract birds. I've seen various directions that have prompted a few improvements. Our way, the feeder will be quite presentable (the garish graphics are painted over) and also more durable than an unpainted carton — it should last through an ordinary winter. It's also easier for birds to use than basic kids' versions because it has perches; and its ballast of gravel or pebbles occupies space that would otherwise need to be filled with food the birds can't possibly reach.

Materials

- *1-quart milk carton, rinsed and dried*
- *Shellac*
- *Spray-on enamel or other durable paint*
- *Gravel or pebbles for ballast*
- *Heavy-duty stapler and staples*
- *Two 6-inch steel skewers with eyes*
- *Strong cord*
- *2 bamboo chopsticks or 7-inch lengths of ¼-inch dowel for perches*
- *A few heavy rubber bands*
- Optional: *Snap for hanging*

Directions

1. Open the top of the milk carton completely and invert the carton over a small can or jar to keep it in place.

ANOTHER FEEDER: THE MILK-CARTON "LOG"

For birds that prefer to cling as they eat, the netting over this recycled carton gives a toehold. Prepare a half-gallon milk carton as described at left to the point of putting in the food. Before doing so, fill part of the carton's center with 2 lengths of cardboard tubing (from paper towels or foil). After filling, don't put in perches — instead, using a long-bladed, narrow knife, cut 2 or 3 round pecking holes about an inch across in each side of the carton. Space the holes well away from the corners. Finally, slip the carton into a recycled onion bag, pulling it to a sung fit. Staple the top of the carton, making sure you secure the netting, too. Rig for hanging as described for the 1-quart feeder — you'll need longer skewers or a longer top rod.

Paint the bottom and all four sides of the carton with a thin coat of shellac. Let dry (an hour should be long enough in most areas), then coat with spray-on enamel of any color you consider appropriate. (We like creamy white.) Let dry overnight or longer, until completely dry to the touch.

2. Fill the bottom of the carton to a depth of an inch or so with small gravel or pebbles, to weight the feeder and reduce the amount of bird food needed to fill it; cover the layer with a pad of folded plastic or foil. Fill the carton to the top crease with plain rendered suet or choose any of the mixtures in the recipe section, the more suety the better. Fold and staple the top shut, using plenty of staples.

3. Pierce the pointed top on each side just under the peak and insert the two 6-inch skewers, one from each side, so a ring sticks out at each end. (Lacking skewers, run a bamboo chopstick or a stiff rod of any kind through the peak.) Rig a hanging loop of strong cord through the skewer eyes or around the ends of the rod, using two or more loops for sturdiness.

4. Pierce one side of the carton, about 2½ inches from the bottom, with the tip of a large nail or an icepick. Push a chopstick or a 7-inch length of dowel through the carton and suet and make a second "starter" hole with the nail where the end of the perch touches the inside; shove the perch through and into final position. Put in a second perch at right angles to the first and about 3 inches above it. To ensure that the perches won't pull out, you might loop a couple of stout rubber bands around the ends of each pair.

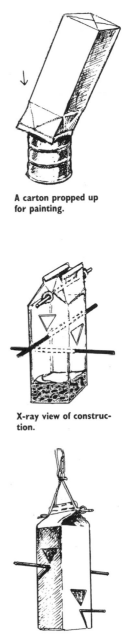

A carton propped up for painting.

X-ray view of construction.

Finished feeder is hung by a cord and a snap.

5. Complete the feeder by cutting a triangular hole about an inch above each perch, with a base about 1 inch wide and a height of about 1¼ inches; or make it round or square and a little over an inch across.

To hang: Gather the top loops together in a metal snap and attach the snap to a stretched hanging line or to a connecting line leading to a tree limb or bracket. (See pages 133–135 for ways and means of hanging feeders.)

To refill: As holes are eaten in the food, it will tend to migrate downward in the feeder. When what's left becomes hard for the birds to get at, trowel more suet mixture through the openings.

Repairs: Overenthusiastic woodpeckers (or squirrels, if they get a chance) may damage the feeder. Just tape up any gashes with strapping tape or duct tape.

STUFFED PINE CONES

A classic for feeding suet-loving birds. Buy or gather good-size pine (or other conifer) cones. Pack their open spaces with the suet-based or peanut butter-based mixture of your choice, or melt rendered suet and pour it repeatedly into and over the cones until all the spaces are filled.

Optionally, roll the filled cones in sunflower meats or black (preferably black-oil) sunflower seeds. Attach loops of wire for hanging. Cones can be refilled when the birds have polished off your first offering.

Myth 10

Metal Feeder Perches or Gratings Can Cause Birds' Feet, Eyes or Tongues to Be Damaged in Freezing Weather

This *may* be possible, but it seems unlikely—experts seem to be saying they've never heard of a genuine case. *Facts:* Birds' feet are armored in dry, horny skin that won't freeze to metal because of its dryness, and birds take good care about where they put their eyes and tongues, just as people do. There you are—prospective Rube Goldbergs who want to make feeders shouldn't shy away from using metal if necessary, although other materials generally look better in the landscape.

Pack suety food into a pine cone, as here, or melt suet and pour it to fill all spaces.

Cake Basket or Suet Box

A n easily made permanent holder, this is good for suet or chunks of any bird bread, cake, corn pone, pudding or other solid food. Don't worry about any possibility of birds being harmed by the metal hardware cloth (see facing page). If you can find plastic-coated hardware cloth, fine; but if not, the ordinary kind does very well.

Materials

- *Piece of hardware cloth, 12 inches square*
- *Piece of ¼-inch or ⅜-inch plywood measuring 6 × 9½ inches*
- *Heavy-duty stapler and staples*

Directions

1. Using tin snips, cut a 3 × 3-inch square out of each corner of the hardware cloth. Then, using a metal straight edge, fold each side upward in line with the cut-out corners, forming the outlines of an open box. You'll have to fold each side flat again before you fold the next side, but once a fold is made it can be reshaped easily by hand. When all sides have been folded and reflattened, turn the piece over and make a second fold, in the opposite direction from the first, midway between the original crease and the edge. Shape all sides into their original folds so you have a box with open flaps.

2. Place the box, open side down, on the piece of plywood. Using a staple gun, fasten the lower flap flat to the board, edges flush; staple right up to the fold

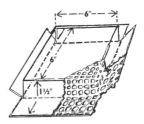

This firmly stapled wire box helps foil predators.

The bark base gives footing to tree-clingers.

of the box. Now refold the side flaps so they lie behind the board and staple them in place.

3. Open the fold at the top end of the box and insert your bird food, then fold the top flap down again. You can leave the flap free, or staple it down (as we do, to foil suet-stealing varmints).

To hang: This feeder can be hung up by means of an eye screw inserted near its top, or it can be tacked to a post or tree.

To refill: When you need to refill the feeder, you need only remove the staples on the top flap and open it wide.

Hanging-Log Feeder

One of the easiest, and in many ways most satisfactory, of bird-feeding arrangements is the feeding log, known to generations of bird-befrienders but worth describing again for any new members of the club. It's a favorite dining spot for all the tree-clinging birds, and some others will also drop in for a bite.

A drilled log is simple to prepare; even better, it looks like part of the natural setting. Raid your own woodpile or a firewood dealer's for a log or tree limb with rough bark so the birds can hang on readily.

Materials

- *Length of rough-barked log or tree limb, 3–4 inches in diameter and 16–20 inches long*
- *Eye screw*
- *Hanging wire*

Directions

1. Drill some holes in the log, each at least an inch in diameter and an inch

---

THE "PLASTERED" BARK-SLAB FEEDER

This permanent wire-faced food bin is designed to hold any of the suety or peanut-buttery puddings, cakes or meatballs, or rendered suet.

Start with a thin slab of log with the bark on, about a foot long and 8 inches wide, or use a rough-sawed board. Nail 1-inch strips of lumber onto the slab to make a rectangle about 6 × 8 inches. Cover the box by nailing or stapling hardware cloth onto the edging. For a more natural look, glue or nail strips of peeled-off bark around the edges to conceal the sides of the wood and to give birds a good foothold.

Fasten a large screw eye to the top of the slab, then fill the food box by pressing through the wire any softened bird food mixture or slightly softened rendered suet. Hang the feeder from a nail driven into a post or tree. Before refilling, it's a sound practice to rinse out any leftover bits of food with hot water.

(or a little more) deep, spaced about 3 inches apart. If making 1-inch holes seems a problem, it isn't, if you have an ordinary ⅜-inch electric drill; hardware stores sell a 1-inch drill bit that will fit it and will make five or six holes in five or six minutes. (Alternatively, if you have a saw but no drill, make a number of coarse diagonal cuts into the bark of the log, making them as wide as you can.) Finally, insert an eye screw into the top end of the log and add a wire for hanging it up; or drive nails into opposite sides of the log near the top and rig a hanging wire between them.

Hanging logs are easy to refill.

2. Pack rendered suet (or any of the suety or peanut-buttery mixtures in the recipe section) into the holes or gashes and hang the log.

To refill: Simply unhook the log and repack it with fresh food, using a rubber spatula or your fingers.

A drilled log slab to fasten to tree or post.

Feeding Table

A feeding table is the prime place for feeding most birds, except for the tree-climbers, who prefer off-the-ground hanging or fixed feeders containing suet or suety mixtures, and some small seedeaters (goldfinches, for instance), who prefer hanging seed holders. At our house cardinals, blue jays, tufted titmice, finches, white-throated sparrows, song sparrows and mourning doves, to name a few, love to dine from low tables, of which we have several.

The table can be any flat surface of suitable size (about 2 by 3 feet is good), placed from 6 inches to 3 feet off the ground. A solid table should have good

FIXED-LOG FEEDER

Use a half-round section of a largish log. Drill and fill the holes as for the hanging-log feeder, then bolt or nail the log to a post at a height convenient for refilling.

drainage (the top can be made to slope to one side, or may have drainage openings) so that during a rainstorm the food neither washes away nor stands in water. However, a screen-topped table like ours solves the drainage problem better than a tilted top. Making one is easy for anyone with a little skill and minimal tools and materials.

On the table go seeds, grains, fruit, nuts and a great miscellany of other things birds will eat — the meat-and-potatoes part of the menu — as well as crumbled-up items of fancier fare (see the recipe section).

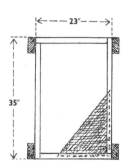

A screen-bottomed table is simple to make and maintain.

Materials

- *Two 22-inch lengths and two 34-inch lengths of 1 × 2-inch common pine stripping*
- *2-inch finishing nails for frame*
- *1 yard of 24-inch window screening, preferably plastic*
- *Heavy-duty stapler and staples*
- *Four 10-inch lengths of 2 × 4 lumber for legs*
- *2½-inch nails for attaching legs*
- Optional: *10 feet of 1-inch wood stripping to make raised edge*

Directions

1. Make a frame by L-butting the pine strips (see sketch) with the 2-inch faces vertical; use 2-inch finishing nails.
2. Staple the screening over the frame, stretching it as taut as possible. *Important:* Begin stapling from the centers of two opposite sides, putting in staples ½ inch apart first on one side and then the other and stretching the screening hard as you go (recruit an extra pair of hands if you can). Staple the other two

sides in the same way. Fold the free edges of the screening down onto the sides of the frame and staple them at close intervals; trim the edges, if you wish. Now you have the top of the table. (For extra top support, cut two crossbars to fit between the sidepieces and nail them in place under the mesh.)

3. To get the table off the ground, simply nail the four 2 × 4s to the frame at each end of the long dimension (see sketch), using 2½-inch nails. You now have a table that's light enough to move around but strong enough to support the squirrels (they are inevitable) as well as birds. After adding legs, you can use it as is or you can nail on a border of narrow wooden strips. There are more professional ways to build a table, but this works. (A table could also be built around a ready-made window screen — really handy persons can visualize the how-to's.)

At ground level a log "table" attracts a range of birds.

Suet Bell

This is a graceful shape made by molding one of the suet-rich bird cakes or puddings in a flowerpot, then unmolding and hanging it in its mesh jacket to provide footing for birds while they peck. Making a suet bell sounds fussier than it is — when you've made one you'll be ready to make more in jig time, perhaps as gifts for birder-friends.

Materials

- *Recycled mesh onion bag*
- *4-inch clay flowerpot*
- *Recycled screw-on bottle cap*

A SPLIT-LOG TABLE

To rig a "table" close to the ground, arrange split logs, any number to suit your space, close together with their flat sides up. Ground birds love rummaging around and under these, and many birds will come to eat on top.

- *Recycled cut-out top of a coffee can or other 4-inch metal disk*
- *Mason's cord or picture wire*
- *Suet mixture of your choice*

Directions

1. Push the closed end of the mesh onion bag through the flowerpot's drainage hole from the inside, leaving enough mesh extending from the pot to fold back over its future contents. Next, take an ice pick in hand and punch a hole through the bottle cap and a hole through the center of the metal disk. Make a firm, fat knot at one end of a 2 foot length of mason's cord or picture wire and thread it through the disk, then through the bottle cap from the inside, then through the drainage hole of the pot, keeping it inside the mesh lining. Pull about a foot of cord through the pot hole and leave it for the time being.

2. Back inside the pot, push the bottle cap snugly against the pot hole; drape the relaxed string connecting the cap with the disk to one side. Pack the pot tightly with your chosen suet mixture, then fold the open ends of the mesh bag over the food; tighten the cord between all the elements by pulling its upper end while you push the disk firmly against the food.

3. Chill the whole works until very firm, then unmold the bell. Before hanging it out, stretch out the surplus mesh at the top and tie it to the hanging cord with wire twists—the mesh "sleeve" makes a good landing spot for birds.

For a truly bell-like shape, you can sculpt the mold a little with a knife dipped in hot water, giving it a curved waist.

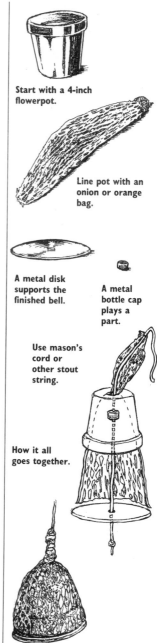

Start with a 4-inch flowerpot.

Line pot with an onion or orange bag.

A metal disk supports the finished bell.

A metal bottle cap plays a part.

Use mason's cord or other stout string.

How it all goes together.

The finished "bell."

Orange, Doughnut or Suet Spike

Food impaled on the spike is easy to reach for a bird on the perch below.

You can buy little wooden sheds designed as hanging shelter for these edibles, or you can employ simple carpentry to make something along the same lines. This version makes use of a slice of log with its own bark attached, more natural-looking than the merchants' models. Lacking a log, a rough-sawed board will do, but it must be thick enough to hold the glued-in pegs securely.

Materials

- *Two 5-inch lengths of 1/4-inch wooden dowel*
- *Log slab with bark on, about 10 inches long and 6 inches wide, or a rough-sawed plank*
- *Woodworker's glue*
- *Eye screw*

Directions

1. Whittle a point on one of the lengths of dowel; leave the second piece unsharpened. Drill a 1/4-inch hole an inch deep into the log just above its midpoint, then drill another hole 3 inches below the first.
2. Using woodworker's glue, fasten the pointed dowel, point outward, into the upper hole and the plain spike into the lower hole. Insert an eye screw into the top surface of the slab so it may be hung from a nail in a tree or post.
3. When the glue job has cured (allow as much time as the label advises), impale half an orange (at any time of year) or, in cool weather, a doughnut, chunk of suet or chunk of suet cake on the sharpened spike.

PLANTING A DOUGHNUT TREE

At tree-pruning time, save a branch (or a large shrub trimming) 4 or 5 feet long that has branchlets stout enough to bear a bird's weight plus a doughnut. "Plant" the pruned piece in late fall, sticking it into the soil in a large tub or pot vacated by summer flowers. There you are — a "tree" on which doughnuts can be spiked and small bags of suet or suety mixtures can be hung.

For better looks, you can landscape around the base of the tree by sticking in evergreen trimmings; this also makes a sheltered rummaging space for such species as white-throated and song sparrows, which like to stay close to the ground.

For the "fruits" of the tree, see Sugared Doughnuts on page 91.

Suet Ball with No Visible Means of Support

A twined-together ball of grapevines or other strong vines is the base of this refillable ball. Make the shape whenever the plant material is at hand—perhaps when fashioning grapevine wreaths to be garnished later as holiday decorations— and complete it by adding food whenever you feel it's time to feast the birds.

Materials

- *Pliable, thin grapevines, leaves and small stems removed*
- *Masking tape, if needed*
- *3-inch metal disk (such as the cutout end of a food can)*
- *18-inch length of picture wire*

Directions

1. If the vine stems are dry, give them a bathtub soaking until they're pliable enough to bend without breaking.

2. Wind them into a loose ball, tucking in the ends when a new piece is attached; if necessary, use masking tape to hold loose ends while you proceed. When it's about the size of a baseball, the vine shape is large enough. If it shows a tendency to unwind, apply masking tape to hold the shape until it has dried, which will take at least a week. (It will keep indefinitely.)

3. Remove any tape from the outside of the ball. Make a hole with an ice pick or screwdriver through the metal disk and make a large knot at one end of the length of picture wire (pliers help).

Suet packed into a grapevine ball is simply replenished by replastering the base.

Thread the wire through the hole in the disk, then work it carefully through the center of the vine ball. Pull the disk and ball together.

4. Soften rendered suet or any suet-based bird food (the puddings, or any of the suet-based cakes) slightly and pack the food firmly into and over the vine ball, plastering it on until you have a solid sphere. Optionally, coat the ball in chopped peanuts, peanut hearts, nutmeats or sunflower meats. Chill until firm.

To hang: Twist a loop in the free end of the wire, attach a snap and hang the suet ball from a stretched feeder line; or attach the wire directly, without the snap, to a tree limb or bracket.

To refill: Shake out any remnants of old food and replaster the ball.

Both popcorn and cranberries make handsome edible garlands.

Grapevine Wreath

A grapevine wreath can be a jolly sight in winter if you add a holiday bow. *Sans* bow, it is a great hit with all our tree-haunting birds, including the shy brown creeper.

Materials

- *Pliable, thin grapevines, leaves and small stems removed*
- *Masking tape*
- *Wire for hanging*

Directions

1. If the vine stems are dry, give them a bathtub soaking until they're pliable enough to bend without breaking.
2. Form a long length of trimmed vine into a circle about 8 inches in diame-

GARLANDS: STOUT THREAD & A BIG NEEDLE

This way of assembling bird food has great possibilities for employing child labor, or for doing pleasant handwork while listening to music or watching TV. Just string unseasoned popcorn or firm cranberries on any length of strong (carpet) thread that suits you — short strings can be tied together later. Or string together some Nutty Popcorn Balls (page 103).

If you like old-time decorations, drape plain popcorn or cranberry strings on your indoor Christmas tree and move them to an outdoor tree or shrub when the holidays are past. Or offer the garlands to the birds in the first place. See page 111 for other items to place on a birds' Christmas tree.

ter. Add more vines to the wreath, twining the new lengths around those in place and tucking in the ends; if necessary, use masking tape to hold them in place. The wreath is large enough when it's 1½ to 2 inches thick. Perfect looks aren't important—this is an underpinning, not an ornament. Let the wreath dry for at least a week. (It will keep until needed, even until next year.)

3. Spread a sheet of plastic wrap on a plate that's a little bigger than the wreath. Lay on the wreath and press slightly softened rendered suet or a rich suet or peanut-butter mixture firmly into the wreath from all the sides you can reach. When you've put on as much as the wreath will hold, cover it with a second piece of plastic and invert the whole assembly onto a second plate. (The plates help hold the shape.) Remove the top plastic and pack the exposed side, then replace the plastic and mold and firm up the wreath with your hands, working from all sides. Optionally, give the finished wreath a coating of sunflower meats, nutmeats, peanuts or peanut hearts. Chill on the plate until firm.

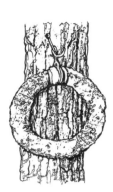

A renewable feast: any suet mixture can be supported by this wreath of grapevines.

To hang: Reinforce a section at the top of the wreath with a winding or two of masking tape, then fasten a couple of large, loose rounds of wire over the tape, twist them close to the tape with pliers and shape the surplus into a hanging loop. Optionally, add a small red weatherproof bow. Hang the wreath from a nail or hook in a tree, post or the side of the house, wherever birds will find it.

To refill: Simply plaster on a fresh supply of the suet mixture of your choice.

Hang It All, or Almost

Holders for foods that can't be served on the feeding table or on the ground should be hung (or post-mounted) in a fashion that doesn't alarm but instead attracts the birds. This means that hanging feeders shouldn't be subject to very much blowing in the wind, which bothers certain species more than others. We've figured out a few ways to steady things down. It's also all to the good if you can foil at least some of the four-footed predators (squirrels, raccoons, opossums) that love to get at eats not meant for them. We have an idea or two on this, also, discussed below among the hanging strategies we've worked out at our house.

If the very idea of doing it yourself gives you a headache, skip all this. Many hanging devices are included in stocks of bird-feeders' supplies and equipment — dealers sell mounting posts in variety, brackets, squirrel baffles and some many-armed rigs that will accommodate a whole set of feeders in a small space.

Line 'Em Up

A strong, stretched line will accommodate a number of hanging items, the total depending on its length — hanging feeders should be spaced 3 or more feet apart on the line. We use heavy monofilament nylon line (a hardware store item), which we've found too thin to let squirrels wire-walk with any ease to the lunch counter. You can also try covered "flex" (which is thicker, and walkable for most squirrels), stainless-steel wire or multistrand picture wire.

Ethereal minstrel!
pilgrim of the
sky!
Dost thou despise
the earth where
cares abound?
Or, while the wings
aspire, are heart
and eye
Both with thy nest
upon the dewy
ground?
—*Wordsworth, "To a*
Sky-Lark"

Stretch the wire as tightly as possible between trees, posts or buildings, or any combination thereof. (Dick, our avian engineer, has installed a turnbuckle from the hardware store at one end of each line in order to tighten up the works when a little sagging sets in.) If the line must be placed where the winds of heaven blow hard, there are ways to prevent or lessen windsway. One way is to rig two parallel lines instead of one; the feeders hang from the upper one and are anchored to the lower one by a second short line. Alternatively, the feeders can be steadied by attaching a guy wire to the bottom of each and securing it to a tent peg (from the camping department) or a sturdy wooden post driven into the ground.

Two or more feeders hanging from a stretched line will tend to converge by sliding. This can be prevented by making "stops" a couple of inches apart where you want each feeder to stay. It's simplest to use fisherman's split lead weights, which you simply crimp onto the line. Or twist several thicknesses of thin wire, or a couple of rounds of a twist tie, around the line and crimp the loops firmly together with pliers.

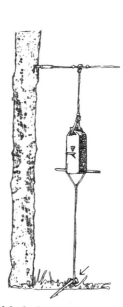

A feeder hanging from a line (keep it taut with a turnbuckle) can be steadied by a tent-peg anchor (above) or a parallel line (below).

Tree Limbs

Branches would be perfect supports for hanging feeders except for the squirrels' penchant for using them as highways to feeding heaven. There are ways to fight back, besides setting up a squirrel-feeding area at a distance from the birds' station and keeping it well stocked with corn (recommendable, in any case).

Baffles: One of the best defenses is placing a squirrel baffle on the line attached to the feeder—this is a dome-shaped plastic gizmo, widely sold.

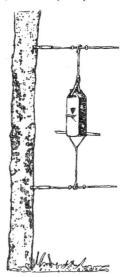

Another defense is hanging "tree" feeders beyond a squirrel's jumping distance from trunk, limb or ground, and hanging them with monofilament line that's difficult or impossible for squirrels to shinny down. Feeders hung this way will afford more comfortable dining if they're anchored to a tent peg, as discussed above.

Brackets

Swiveling brackets that extend at right angles from house, shed, fence or tree are widely sold. However, you need only rudimentary carpentry skills to make a fixed bracket from scrap wood (see sketch).

For hanging a feeder from a bracket, we recommend the ever-useful monofilament line or metal picture wire; the first is hard for beasties to grip and the second is also hard to grip *and* hard to bite through if a raider should get his teeth into it.

A baffle may be desirable on the hanging line — it depends on where you live, and just which creatures share your environment.

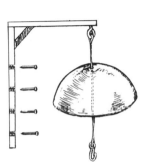

Food hung from a home-built bracket can be shielded from squirrels by a transparent plastic baffle.

Good Reading When Not Bird Watching

◆

The card catalog of any library worthy of its Dewey decimal system will list books on bird identification, behavior and feeding, and on fostering birds by creating habitat. Established names in these fields include, in no particular order (and in addition to peerless Roger Tory Peterson, in a class by himself): John K. Terres, Shirley L. Scott, Paul R. Ehrlich, Kevin Zimmer, Arthur C. Bent, John Bull, W. E. Godfrey, Hal H. Harrison, John V. Dennis, George Harrison and Kit Harrison, Alan Pistorius, Stephen W. Kress, Christopher Leahy, Donald W. Stokes and Lillian Q. Stokes, Ralph Palmer, and H. C. Oberholser.

When in search of a field guide, you can't go wrong with any of those that follow, although their strengths vary and it's a good idea to have a look before making a choice. Some are illustrated with paintings, some with photographs, some with both; the range maps vary in size and clarity; and information on bird songs and habits is rendered in various ways. We own several of those listed, plus some less authoritative bird books, and use

❝*He's in great want of a bird that will give a groat for an owl.***❞**
—*John Ray,*
English Proverbs

them vigorously when we're doubtful about just which feathered friend we're looking at.

Field Guides

New editions of these guides are to be expected from time to time; the latest available edition will reflect new observations and recent changes in bird classifications and names.

The Audubon Society Field Guide to North American Birds: Eastern Region, by John Bull and John Farrand, Jr. Companion volume, subtitled *Western Region,* by Miklos D. F. Udvardy. Knopf (New York). Illustrated with bird photographs.

The Audubon Society Master Guide to Birding, edited by John Farrand, Jr. Three volumes. Knopf (New York). Illustrated with both photos and paintings. Our first choice among bird guides, but rather bulky for toting outdoors.

Birds of North America, by Chandler S. Robbins, Bertel Bruun and Herbert S. Zim. Golden Press (New York). Illustrations are paintings.

Field Guide to the Birds of North America. The National Geographic Society (Washington, D.C.). Illustrated with paintings.

Peterson Field Guide Series. Volumes on birds, by Roger Tory Peterson, cover eastern and central North America, the West, Texas and adjacent states, and Mexico. Houghton Mifflin (Boston).

As a supplement to field guides, we recommend the *The Birder's Handbook: A Field Guide to the Natural History of North American Birds,* by Paul R. Ehrlich, David S. Dobkin and Darryl Wheye. Simon & Schuster (New York), 1988. Intended as a supplement to identification guides, this

❝*The bird-watcher's life is an endless succession of surprises.***❞**
—*William Henry Hudson,* The Book of a Naturalist

handbook is keyed to the National Geographic, Golden, Peterson and Audubon guides and is highly recommended both for its detail on species (it goes far beyond the limits imposed by identification guides) and for its wealth of background and behavioral information; it's an all-you-ever-wanted-to-know compendium.

Regional Guides

For information on bird guides for your area that will let you know which birds you may be able to attract, write to:

The American Birding Association
P.O. Box 6599
Colorado Springs, CO 80934

Regional guides are also carried by the Crow's Nest Book Shop, the gift shop of Cornell's ornithology lab. For a catalog write to the address given below.

Periodicals

The Living Bird Quarterly
Laboratory of Ornithology
Cornell University
159 Sapsucker Woods Road
Ithaca, NY 14850

Birder's World
720 East 8th Street
Holland, MI 49423

Bird Watcher's Digest
P.O. Box 110
Marietta, OH 45750

WildBird
P.O. Box 6040
Mission Viejo, CA 92690

Audubon and *American Birds*
Audubon Society
950 Third Avenue
New York, NY 10022

Is it for thee the lark ascends and sings?
Joy tunes his voice, joy elevates his wings.
Is it for thee the linnet pours his throat?
Loves of his own and raptures swell the note.
— Pope, An Essay on Man, *Epistle III*

Index

(Page numbers in **boldface** refer to
main entries in the bird list.)